HiLARIE
MAKE E[
AWE3ME

ONE
TEAM
ONE
DREAM

For Rck
Joey Sigar

ONE
TEAM
ONE
DREAM

**Indispensable Teamwork Skills
to Create a Collaborative Culture**

GREGG GREGORY

Copyright © 2016 Kensington, Maryland
Office: 301-564-0908
E-mail: Gregg@TeamsRock.com
Website: WWW.TeamsRock.com

For additional information, printable versions of the forms used in this book, and more tips and tools to promote a winning team culture, visit http://bonuses.teamsrock.com

ISBN-978-0-9961239-2-1

Printed in the United States

PROJECT MANAGER: John Peragine • info@osiris-papers.com

Contents

Chapter 1 - The Journey to a Great Team   **T•1**

Let's Get Our Bearings   T•2

One Ship — One Course   T•3

The Perspective of a Six-Year-Old   T•4

Three Zones of Life   T•6

Which Zone Do You Typically Operate In?   T•9

Success Begins with Trust   T•10

Chapter 2 - The Anatomy of an Effective Team   **T•13**

Definition of Team   T•13

The Four Stages of Team Matriculation   T•19

Which Stage Is Your Team In Right Now?   T•26

Myths about Effective Teams   T•27

Team Player Thinking   T•30

Chapter 3 - Behaviors in an Effective Team   **T•33**

Followership   T•34

What Type of Follower Are You?   T•35

Four Traits of Effective Team Members   T•38

The A.B.E. Effect — Awareness Brings Effectiveness   T•41

Awareness Exercise   T•42

10 Little Words…   T•43

Chapter 4 – Communicating Effectively   **T•47**

Everything DiSC®   T•47

The Three V's   T•50

Don't Judge a Wrestler by his Tattoos   T•52

The United States Powerboat Show   T•53

Communication by Phone   T•55

E.T.R.D.   T•55

Accomplishments Log   T•58

Chapter 5 – Working Through Conflict with a Teammate   **T•59**

Three Stages of Conflict   T•60

Conflict Management Style Survey   T•64

The Five Conflict Resolution Styles   T•68

Using R.E.S.P.E.C.T. to Work Through Conflict   T•69

It is only the Beginning…   T•71

The material in this book is just the beginning of your journey.
You can find more information, workbook pages, and tools on
http://bonuses. teamsrock.com

I want to thank my mom and my dad for adopting me and taking the time to raise me with love and values. Mom, you gave me compassion, and Dad, you gave me my stick-to-it-tiveness.

How to Use This Book

When I began the journey of this book, I thought about how I could create one book that looked at both sides of the equation of teamwork and leadership. It seemed hard to incorporate it all into a single book, but at the same time, I really didn't want to create two, as that would separate the connection that unifies teams and leaders. Thus, this unique book and concept was born.

In essence, this is really two books smashed into one. Each half of the book contains stories, models, exercises and advice that I have gathered and used in my presentations, keynotes and workshops for years. It is the best-of-the-best of my material that has helped both teams and leaders alike, ultimately helping to inspire an extraordinary culture.

After thinking about the order of the two halves and having a lot of conversations with my clients, I decided that the team half should be read first, because all great leaders need to understand teamwork and followership and you don't have to be a great leader to be a great team member. That is not to say that team members would not gain valuable information from the leader half. In fact, I encourage everyone to read both halves of this book. It is the order of the reading that is important.

Over the last 20 years of working with teams, one of the most common comments I receive is, "Are our managers getting this same information?" This book is designed to get everyone on the same page and moving in one direction — One Team, One Dream.

Once you have finished reading the team half of this book, continue on and read the leader half. It is important that teams and leaders are on the same page - that they have a single vision and a clear understanding of one another. Teams and leaders are two sides of one coin; it is only when they forget this that things can go awry. There has to be an unwavering bond between the two in order for the leader to be effective and the team to be productive and efficient.

Chapter 1 The Journey to a Great Team

Great teams don't just happen in a vacuum. They take work, dedication, and did I mention work? This is a long journey with significant ports-of-call, and there is no final destination. It is a journey of continual growth and evolution. The journey to a great team may be a confusing title for this chapter, because it implies a destination that a team reaches, where they finally "gel." The reality is that a great team evolves during the journey and becomes more cohesive with each leg of the journey and each challenge they face together. A team cannot know their strength without being tested, which means that they will be challenged along the way. Each challenge is an opportunity for reflection, maturity, and growth.

I have a journey as well, and that is to help leaders and teams work together in harmony and strength. In order to clearly illustrate that point, I developed the anagram **TEAMS ROCK**, because that is the center of my journey.

At the end of each half of the book, you will see **TEAMS ROCK**, and I wanted to offer it here, at the beginning of the journey, so that when you reach the end, it will be a reminder.

T   Success begins with **TRUST**
E   Results "happen" with **ENGAGEMENT**
A   Mutual **ACCOUNTABILITY**
M   Passion for the **MISSION**
S   **SYNCHRONIZE** across lines

R   Focus on **RESULTS**
O   100% **OWNERSHIP** of actions
C   **CULTURE** is core
K   Share your **KNOWLEDGE**

This is the foundation of what I do with my clients to help them build better and more efficient teams. In this half of the book, we will cover each of these concepts, utilizing the same material I offer my audiences — so you have a complete playbook that I have never given to any of my audiences in its entirety. You will be given the tools you need to become part of a team of ROCK STARS — whether you are team member or team leader. Remember, we are all in this together.

✳ Let's Get Our Bearings

Before any successful journey, it is best to get your bearings, to figure out where you are and where you intend to go.

Think about a ship - you have a captain, and then there is the crew. On larger ships, this could mean there are officers between the captain and the crew. Remember, there is only one captain, even if he or she has a first or second mate. Each has a defined job, and both must have an understanding of, and respect for, the other. The ultimate responsibility of what happens to the ship and crew lies with the captain. The captain must navigate the ship to its destination. He or she must chart a course, and avoid storms, because lives depend on it. The captain has to make decisions based upon the support and feedback of his or her crew, and while he or she may listen to the input of the crew, the captain ultimately makes the final decision.

The crew has various duties on the ship that fall into various categories — engine room, mess hall, armory, security, etc. The reality is that everyone is on one ship and, in order to get to the desired destination, they need to work together.

Corporations are like ships. They need both confident, strong leaders and crews that are dedicated to doing their jobs together to move the ship, or organization, from one destination to the next. It is up to the leader to lead the crew, and it is just as important that the crew do their part to work together and follow the leader's guidance.

🧭 One Ship — One Course

A team (crew) must be given orders or guidance and direction to know what to do, when to do it, and for what purpose. Like the captain of a ship, a team leader must know the course in order to get the crew (team) to their destination safely and efficiently. Today GPS, or Global Positioning Satellites, are used to help captains navigate their course. This book is a GPS device for both team members and team leaders alike.

It has only been within the last couple of decades that we have used electronic devices to get around, bouncing signals off of satellites in space. When was the last time you opened up a paper map, or plotted a course using an almanac?

For those 30 or under, an almanac is a big book full of colorful maps and pictures that are often obsolete as soon as you buy them because they don't auto-update. Can you imagine?

Before there were maps, or even compasses, people made their way by looking to the sky, to the stars, to guide their way. There was one star that shone bright in the sky and was a constant: the North Star or Polaris, as it is astronomically known. Sea captains were able to set and adjust their courses by this star.

With each generation, a new technology was born that made navigation a bit easier. I am still waiting for the machine that just transports your molecules and reassembles you somewhere else, but I may have to wait a bit for that luxury.

The point is that as we learn more, navigation becomes easier. This book was created to help navigate you and your team to become an effective team more quickly and easily by following the pathways set forth in this guide.

I am going to challenge you a bit, because I don't want you to have just any ole' experience. I want this journey to becoming a part of an effective team to be different. In order to become something new, you have to begin thinking differently.

As I already mentioned, it is not the journey, but how the team comes together to overcome challenges — both externally (with the people the team serves) and internally (there are a number of internal challenges that can impact the integrity of a team). The only way for a team to make positive changes and realize outcomes that are different is to look around and try to see things from new and different perspectives. The difficulty is that many of us become complacent and too comfortable — and contradictory to the old adage, even old dogs can learn new tricks. The "trick" is that you and your team will have to want to elicit positive change. It is up to every team member to work in harmony to achieve the agreed-upon goals. One person cannot dictate a team.

When whitewater rafting, it takes everyone in the boat paddling in sync to move the boat smoothly through the rapids. If just one person is not synchronized in their paddling, the boat may spin, or worse, dump the folks in the boat. Everyone has to work together in the same direction.

I have found from my keynotes and programs that people respond positively to stories that illustrate points rather than me just lecturing to my audience. I have chosen my best real-life stories to share with you throughout both halves of this book. (All the names have been changed to protect the guilty!)

Let me share with you the perspective of youth - innocent, unburdened, and open to all possibilities. We lose this perspective as we mature, when we layer ourselves with definitives, static beliefs and values. I want you to be open to different ways of looking at your team and your purpose within your team.

The Perspective of a Six-Year-Old

After my father died, I was still friends with some of his old cronies. One day, I went over to help my dad's friend Dan clean out his rain gutters. He was about eighty years old, and he didn't really want to climb up the ladder and get on the roof. Since his son lived about four hours away, he asked if I could come over on that Saturday morning and help him because we were expecting a rainstorm.

I got over to Dan's house by 8:00, climbed up the ladder and cleaned the gutters. There were a lot of leaves and other not-so-pleasant things in there. It felt good helping out an old friend. The work took me about 90 minutes, and when I finished the work, we sat on the porch, relaxed, and chatted a bit. After about an hour, he excused himself and said he wanted to get some checks in the mail before the letter carrier came by. He went to the hall closet and pulled out a vintage portable Smith Corona typewriter. You know what I'm talking about, the one that came in its own little briefcase. He explained that his hands were too shaky to write the checks. It was just simpler to type them out and sign them.

While he was typing out the checks, I began packing my stuff to head home when his daughter dropped by and his six-year-old grandson, Ethan, came running in the door.

Dan was concentrating on typing each letter with one finger. His grandson came over and looked at his grandfather with a peculiar look. Now, I expected him to say, "What's that?" or something to that effect.

Not a chance. Instead, he said, "Hey Grandpa, that's cool. You don't even have to wait for the printer to warm up." Now that is seeing something from an entirely different perspective.

Have you been doing something for so long at work that it is second nature? You no longer think about it, nor do you see a need to try to do it differently. Have you been doing something for so long that you are in a rut? Try to look at what you are doing with the eyes of Dan's grandson. Look at your process and how you interact with others on your team. If something does not seem to be working, look at it from a different perspective and the answer may be clear. Whether you are a frontline worker or a senior leader, you have to push yourself off of the sofa of your life. Change does not occur in the lap of apathy.

Begin to challenge your way of thinking. Open your mind to the new possibilities and perspectives I am offering. Become that six-year-old child, full of wonder, with a unique and creative perspective on the world. You must be willing to look at yourself hard in the mirror and decide what kind of team member you are and what type of team member you want to be.

In order to determine whether you are in a rut in your thinking or behavior, I present the Three Zones of Life. These are the places we find ourselves in life. They are not necessarily progressive in a linear way. In fact, we shift in and out of these zones at different times in our lives. This is part of knowing where you are in order to determine where you are headed.

✸ Three Zones of Life

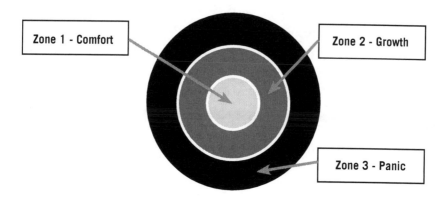

To be part of an effective team, you must first do some self-exploration. It begins with understanding how you operate. Let's explore the three zones of life that every one of us has in common.

Zone 1: Comfort Zone

The comfort zone is where we get our daily activities done: the way we get dressed, the drive to work, how we like our coffee or martini (shaken, not stirred, thank you), the things we do day in and day out. In short, these are the things we do not have to think about and with which we are most comfortable.

We all know people who might plan their day in advance, then arrive at the office or job site so inflexible that even the slightest little hiccup causes them to panic and lose focus.

These are people who live in their comfort zones. Their comfort zones may be very small and subsequently insulated by an equally small growth zone.

Zone 2: Growth Zone

Our growth zone is where we stretch our minds a bit. Let's try an exercise I frequently use in my programs:

1. Use the boxes below or simply draw two boxes in the middle of a blank sheet of paper.

2. Sign your name in the first box – do not print it - sign it as if you were signing a legal document.

```
┌─────────────────────────────────────────────────────┐
│                                                       │
│                                                       │
└─────────────────────────────────────────────────────┘
```

3. Easy to do, right? This is your comfort zone.

4   Now, in the second box, sign your name again, using your other or non-dominant hand

```
┌─────────────────────────────────────────────────────┐
│                                                       │
│                                                       │
└─────────────────────────────────────────────────────┘
```

5. How did you feel about that? This was much more of a challenge for you, right? I can almost hear you moaning and groaning. No whining allowed.

In my seminars and workshops, I ask, "How hard was that?"

People often respond, "It was very hard."

While it is hard, at least you tried. You did try it, didn't you? This simple exercise moves you into your growth zone. Are you willing to become creative and try new things while being a part of the group? Are you willing to grow with others?

Do you know someone who has even moderate turmoil in their day and yet is able to maintain his or her composure? Here is someone who understands and lives a great deal of his or her life in a growth zone.

Several years ago, I was delivering a workshop in Southfield, Michigan and had the group do this exercise. One of the women in the audience took her pen, threw it down, sat back in her chair, crossed her arms, and defiantly said, "That's stupid. I'm not going to do it."

Where did I send her? That simple activity sent her to the third zone, the panic zone.

Zone 3: Panic Zone

Her defiance told me a lot about her and her behavior style, which we will explore later in the book. What does her response tell you?

* Does she like to delegate?
* When she does delegate, how do you think she does it?
* Do you think she micromanages?
* When she is delegated a task, how well do you think she likes being micromanaged?
* Do you think she likes to work with others, or prefers to work alone?
* What about her personal quality of work?

I asked myself these questions and concluded the following:

* She probably does not like to delegate, because no one can do it as well as she can.
* When she does – she tends to micromanage, due to a lack of trust in the other person's skills.
* She cannot stand being micromanaged; it means that someone is challenging her work.
* She prefers to work alone, because others simply get in her way.
* She personally produces a high quality of work.

Do you know people like this on your team? Are you like this?

Some people live in their comfort zones. For them, it's such a tiny little zone that they have an equally small growth zone. Consequently, they have a massive panic zone.

There was a time when I delivered a keynote speech to 300 people in Atlanta about this subject. There is a difference between 'cannot' and 'will not.' One of the participants said he "could not" do the exercise, and the reason was that he was missing his left arm, below the elbow. He literally could not do the task, so I told him to write his name backwards with his right hand. This is different from the woman above who said she "would not" do it. One is defiance and the other is a limitation. Sometimes we say we cannot when we are really saying that we will not. Be careful to recognize the difference. We limit ourselves with these self-imposed illusions. How do you limit yourself?

Why do we limit ourselves by saying we cannot do something? Many times, it is fear of failure. Fear of embarrassment. Fear of trying. We are all afraid of something in our lives. The question becomes: what are we doing to remove that limitation?

As an effective team member, you do not want to live in a very small comfort zone, thus causing a very large panic zone. When people live in their comfort zone, they often gravitate to their panic zone when asked to do something that they have not tried or, more importantly, are afraid to attempt.

The idea is to live in your growth zone as much as possible, as this will actually expand your comfort zone and help you to avoid the panic zone as much as possible. It is important to understand that you will never eliminate your panic zone, but you can make it smaller by living in your growth zone on a regular basis.

✸ Which Zone Do You Typically Operate In?

The key to adapting to other zones is awareness. Make a concerted effort to exist in your growth zone, so that when stress and emotions are high, you can be creative and your cool head will prevail.

One way to begin moving more into your growth zone is to drive different routes to and from work on a regular basis. You will be surprised at what you see differently.

Understand this: you must live your life in your growth zone and teach others to do the same. Even as a team member, you can help others around you grow. One of the best ways to teach is by example.

I want to emphasize the importance of trust within the team and the importance of trust between the team and the leader. Without trust, the team will quickly slide into bickering, infighting and sabotage. Trust is a two-way street, and we will talk more about trust in the leader half of the book.

✻ Success Begins with Trust

> *"My grandfather once told me that there are two kinds*
> *of people: those who do the work and those who take*
> *the credit. He told me to try to be in the first group;*
> *there was much less competition there."*
>
> - INDIRA GANDHI, THE PRIME MINISTER OF INDIA

To realize success, team members need to recognize their individual responsibilities. Think about the ship analogy from earlier in the chapter. A ship has a defined space and size, and every inch of it is engineered for efficiency. If you have ever been on a ship like an aircraft carrier, you will have a greater understanding of what I am talking about. Aircraft carriers are essentially floating cities without any room for expansion. Every inch, from floor to ceiling, is well thought out and utilized. There is no wasted space. This efficiency also creates a limit on the number of people who exist on the ship. Every position is carefully thought out and necessary. Everyone aboard a smoothly running ship, such as an aircraft carrier, has a job and performs it on time, with precision, and in harmony with others doing their assigned jobs. If you are only taking up space - then you are only eating up necessary resources. Everyone must know what their job is and be clear about what is expected of them.

My father served aboard the U.S. Army Hospital Ship Dogwood during WWII. He was clear about what his job was and loved it. Dad's family owned a small town bakery during the depression, and onboard the Dogwood, he was in charge of baking bread and pastries for the crew and the patients. If you are sent below to the kitchen, there are many things that you could do, but why are you there? Are you there to peel potatoes or chop coconuts? You have to be clear, or again, you will just be taking up space and getting in other people's way. Do you know anyone like that? Do they just seem lost? Is it you?

There is nothing worse than being thrust into a department without a clear understanding of your responsibilities. It is not just the leader's job to tell you; it is also your responsibility to ask. This is something that new hires often encounter. The purpose of this book is to get both the leadership and the frontline moving toward the same goal and in the same direction.

In corporations, there is a responsibility toward the final result. There has to be a purpose to what you are doing. Having a strong understanding of your purpose is important for your job performance and is essential when you are trying to figure out where you fit within your team. If you are rowing left and your team is paddling to the right, your ship may run aground.

Each team member has a responsibility to his or her team members, as well as to the organization, to work together in sync and harmony with other team members. Teams are collections of moving parts, and they all must move in sync to harness their contributions and reach their goal. When these parts or members work against each other, they lose momentum and become ineffective, at which point they're too costly to maintain and more expensive than they're worth.

Next is a team member's responsibility to his or her leader, which is mutual trust and respect. You must believe in the leader's ability to lead, and even if you don't always agree with him or her, you should disagree respectfully, and follow his or her direction. The exception is if the leader is asking you to do something illegal or immoral. If that is the case, you have some serious decisions to make about your position on that particular team, because when a leader asks his or her team to perform such tasks, he or she is not showing mutual respect.

I had a conference attendee come up to me after a presentation and tell me that his boss had told him to outright lie to a customer about when something would be in stock. That employee felt ill when he went to tell the customer. About eight weeks later, I received an email that he had left that company and was now in a much happier place.

There must be respect and trust for the leader in place on the team. One dissenting voice can poison a crew. This does not mean that the person gets the boot; it means that the leader may need to talk to that person. Maybe he or she is not feeling heard or does not feel respect from teammates. If you are the dissenting voice, do you not owe it to the leader to sit down and talk about it?

There have been many studies over the years that have talked about the reasons employees decide to leave a team, department, or company. The vast majority of these studies show that many decisions to leave are based around the team member's relationships with colleagues and managers. This doesn't mean you have to agree with everything leaders say - it just means you have to treat them, in public and private, with respect. Respect is not transactional; it is the right thing to do in all situations. Just because someone does not show you respect does not mean you should respond with disrespect. It means you need to hold on to your integrity, speak your piece, and leave if you need to.

As a team member, you have a responsibility to be the best "you" every day when you arrive at work. As the old saying goes, "A chain is only as strong as its weakest link." When a team member is unable to perform his or her role, the entire mission of the team is in jeopardy. If a team member is confused about his or her role, unhappy about his or her personal reward or motivation, or even experiencing personal issues that invade the team space, he or she is operating at a diminished capacity and could put the team's goals in jeopardy.

Chapter 2 The Anatomy of an Effective Team

There are certain characteristics of effective teams that are universal. There are certain habits that, when applied to a team, help everyone work more cohesively.

When a doctor goes to school to learn his or her trade, one of the classes is always anatomy and physiology, which is required early in medical education. It is a class that breaks the body down into systems and parts so that when a professor mentions an ulna, everyone will know what that is, where it is located, and how it functions. For you non-medical types, the ulna is the thinner and longer of the two bones in the human forearm, on the side opposite the thumb.

In this chapter, we'll break down the parts of an effective team and learn how a team comes together and functions.

✳ Definition of Team

In order to begin properly analyzing the components of a team, it is best that I begin with my definition of an effective team:

A group that trusts and respects each other and:

✳ Possesses harmonizing skills
✳ Has conflict around ideas to maximize dialogue
✳ Is committed to a unified mission
✳ Pursues performance objectives or the mission via an agreed-upon course
✳ Holds each member accountable

Let's break this down. The foundation of any team is trust and respect — and without these as the foundation, teamwork will be an uphill battle. I recall what my father used to say when I was in the 2nd grade: "You cannot put the roof on a house until the foundation is solid and complete." At the time, I had no idea what he meant. As I got older and understood the analogy of "foundation" for everything in life, his words made complete sense.

Think about all the types of teams out there. Beyond the realm of sports teams, what other types of teams come to mind? Jot them down here before moving on. Try to think differently — out of the box, if you will.

Here are just a few teamwork groups, although you might not have thought of them as such:

* A band
* Family
* Church groups and choirs
* Medical emergency room or operating room staffs
* Geese – (studies show they can actually fly 87% further in groups than if they were to fly solo)
* Restaurant staff (kitchen, server)
* NASCAR pit crew.
* Military Blue Angels or Thunderbirds or the Army Golden Knights
* Animal packs –wolves and lions in particular
* Bees, ants and other insects that work together
* Youth gangs
* Organized crime
* Terrorist groups
* Homeowners' Associations
* (Your Team Here)

Naturally, there are many more teams that we can think of, and I encourage you to sit down with your team and brainstorm them to see how many you can come up with.

In order for a team to really function together, there has to be trust between team members. In the other half of this book, I will discuss how a leader can foster this. For now, I would like to emphasize that each member has to not only know his or her role, but also understand how he or she fits within the team. What must you do in order for others to do their jobs well? What do others need to do in order for you to do your job well?

You have to trust that everyone around you is doing what they need to do. You do not have control over that, but you do have control over doing your job so that other people on your team will trust that they can count on you. This is where I trust John enough to share personal information with him, trusting that he will not at some point use that information against me.

During the 2012 Olympics, the men's Jamaican 4x100 meter relay team not only won the race, but they also set a world record of 36.84 seconds. The previous record was 37.04 seconds. The relay race is really four 100-meter dashes tied together with three passes, or hand-offs, of a baton. The world record for the 400-meter dash, which is a race in which a single runner runs 400 meters, was set in 2009 by Michael Johnson with a time of 43.18 seconds. Most people would assume that one sprinter could run faster than four sprinters passing a baton. In actuality, you have four sprinters running 100 meters, and so they do not run out of steam as quickly. The truly amazing part is how these four people worked as a team and were completely synchronized in their handoffs. By the way — even the 7th place team in the 2012 Olympics had a time (38.43) that was significantly better than the world record for the 400-meter dash, illustrating that teamwork works.

A team can work much more efficiently and effectively when they work together. In the relay race, it is all about the handoff. There are so many things that can go wrong, like the handoff of the baton between runners. The next runner in a relay begins running with the current runner for 10 meters (the Acceleration Zone) to match their speed, and the baton must be passed within a 20-meter zone called the Handoff Zone or the team is disqualified. Everything has to be done with precision. There can be no mistakes. When it works, like it did for Jamaica in 2012, the results are phenomenal. How well is your team running? Is someone dropping the baton? Are you dropping the baton?

In business, handoffs are equally essential, whether between team members or between departments. If someone drops the baton, it affects everybody. An example of this is when I worked in the mortgage banking industry. After someone purchased a home, a real estate agent would hand off the buyer to a mortgage loan originator to complete the mortgage application. The loan originator would complete the application and then hand it off to a processor, who ordered the property appraisal and then verified the data provided. The processor would then make sure that all of the documents were correct and all of the necessary supporting documentation was attached.

In some cases, the processor would send the file back to the originator for additional information. The originator would find the information and then pass it back to the processor, who would review the information and then hand off the file to an underwriter for final approval.

The underwriter would review the file, and if the information was in compliance, the loan could be approved. At this point, the underwriter would return the file to the processor, who would make sure that everything was in order before handing off the file to the loan-closing department. The loan-closing department would then prepare the proper legal documents and hand off the paperwork to the settlement attorney, who handled the loan closing and recorded the documents at the courthouse. If anyone dropped the baton, or didn't pass it off correctly, it could mean a delay in closing or result in the loan not being approved. It wasn't the responsibility of just one person or department; it was every person's responsibility to pass information correctly, and with precision, to the next person in the process.

Handoffs occur every day in every industry. In construction, when workers are preparing a foundation, there is a team that pours the concrete, one that sets the studs, another that does electricity, another that does the plumbing, and so on. Everyone relies on the work being done properly and the baton being passed on time. You don't want plumbers to be working on pipes in the same crawl space with electricians. The work has to be properly transitioned from one team or individual to another. When those handoffs don't work correctly, teamwork breaks down, productivity fails, trust erodes, conflict erupts, and commitments are breached.

One of the keys to a great handoff with sprinters is that not a lot of time is spent in the Handoff Zone, the area in which a baton has to be passed to the next sprinter. For boys' high school teams, the goal is 2.2 seconds, and for girls' teams, 2.6 seconds. Think about that. A baton is transferred almost in the blink of an eye while both sprinters are in motion.

Communication on a team is essential to make a smooth pass, and there are sometimes issues that can arise to create a delay or a missed pass. In the 4x100 relay, teams often have an emergency word. This word is spoken if the receiver needs to slow down because the passer does not believe the pass is going to take place in the zone. Both runners are running with everything they have, but they must also make that pass in the 20-meter zone. If they do not, the team is disqualified. It is better to slow down the process a little bit than to be knocked out of the race. Allow me to repeat this – it is better to slow down the process a little bit than to be knocked out of the race.

Sometimes, a team member will complain that he or she cannot do their job because he or she is not receiving the handoff smoothly. The problem is that the team member is often talking to the wrong person about it; he or she should be talking directly to the person making the pass. The two have to work out their communication issues or the whole process, and the team, will falter. In the leader half of the book, we will talk about the role of the coach, aka "team leader," in making sure that everyone is communicating and handoffs are flawless.

It is all about mindset. If the person passing work to another member of the team wants to show off, he or she might blow right past the receiver and ultimately sabotage the handoff. Passers must have the mindset that they trust the receivers explicitly and trust that they are ready to receive the handoff. The receivers must be focused and ready for the handoff. If they slow down, or are not ready, there can be an oversight or misstep and the handoff will not happen properly.

In the 2008 Olympics in Beijing, both the US men's and women's 400 meter relay teams were disqualified during the semifinal 4x100 relays because each team had missteps and dropped a baton. It happens sometimes, even to the best teams. In business, it is not the dropping of the baton that defines a team; it is how quickly they can pick it up and begin running again.

How is your team running? How are you passing along work to your teammates? How are they receiving it?

The team has to move forward together, in sync, and with every member working in cooperation with everyone else. When two people are rowing a boat, they have to decide to paddle in the same direction.

If one is paddling forward and the other in the opposite direction, the boat will just turn in circles. Does this circular pattern seem familiar on your team? Do you feel like you are working against other team members and going nowhere? While the leader sets the direction, the team members must all paddle in a unified direction in order to succeed.

What happens when a boat keeps spinning in circles? People get sick, right? You just want to get off of the boat. In business, this results in team members becoming "sick and tired," so that conflict and, eventually, abnormal turnover often occur. While a leader can help set the direction, it is really up to the team to make it work.

You may be on a team that just formed, or one that has been working together for some time. If you are new to a team, then you may not be aware that teams go through stages. Like the Three Zones of Life, the stages may not be linear in time, and teams tend to shift in and out of these stages.

The Four Stages of Team Matriculation

> *"Before you know where you're going, you must know where you are; before you know where you are, you must know from whence you came."*
>
> —GREGG GREGORY

In 1965, Bruce Tuckman, Professor Emeritus of Educational Psychology at Ohio State University, published his Tuckman's Stages of Group Development. He proposed that there are four main stages that most teams go through — from forming the team to growing the team to becoming a well-oiled machine. I like to call this The Four Stages of Team Matriculation:

* Forming
* Storming
* Norming
* Performing

T•20   Gregg Gregory

I continue to be amazed at the number of high-ranking leaders and business executives who have never seen this concept. Recognizing these stages is critical at every level of an organization to increase teamwork and collaboration.

It is important for you, and the other members of your team, to understand which stage you are in, because each has its own unique set of challenges and strategies. A leader's main task is to help guide you through the four stages. I will talk more about that in the leader half of this book. For now, consider each stage and share with the other members of your team to determine first where you are, then where you want to go, and finally, how you might arrive at that next stage.

Keep in mind that these teams may be permanent teams or simply project teams brought together for a specific task or assignment.

Stage 1: Forming

Like it sounds — forming most often happens when a team first comes together. At this stage, everyone is feeling one another out and getting to know one other. They are not sure of the rules yet, and they don't understand the purpose of the team or the team's direction. Team members may ask many questions like:

* "Why are we doing this?"
* "What's the purpose of this?"
* "Who's responsible for this?"

A strong team leader will listen to your questions to identify where your team happens to be. It is important to trust your leader and be comfortable enough to ask for guidance in any of these stages.

The second key element that applies under forming is a critical one. Team members need ground rules and expectations. In many business cases, team members can, and should, establish these ground rules rather than relying solely on the leader to do it for the team. It is also important that these rules do not violate any larger organizational rules.

If you have ever had a teenager, you will understand this next analogy. Most parents give their teenagers a curfew.

"You must be home by 11."

They may answer, "But Dad, Jim has a later curfew."

Is it okay for Jim's parents to have a different curfew? Absolutely.

Jim's family just has different ground rules, and those ground rules can be different from yours. Remember, your ground rules are your ground rules.

In business, the ground rules should be very simple and established up front. Ground rules have to be established so that the team knows how to work together. Now, their ground rules can be different from another team's ground rules as long as they are congruent with those of the overall organization—the mission, vision, and values.

Ground Rules

Wrigley Field in Chicago has something that no other Major League Baseball field has: ivy that is in play on the outfield wall. If the ball is caught in the ivy, the player has to put both hands up in the air, which signals that the ball is caught in the ivy. The umpire signals a ground rule double and the play is dead.

If your kids have played baseball or softball with an umpire, they go over the rules before the start of every game. Suppose, for instance, that there's a tree hanging over the area of play. The umpire will designate which rule will apply if a ball hits the tree. While the tree may be rooted out of play, the branches may be in play, so it is important that the rules be explicitly stipulated.

In the game of Monopoly,™ you put $500 in the middle of the board at the beginning of each game. If you land on Chance, you draw a card. If it reads, "Pay a poor tax of $15," you put $15 in the middle of the board. Somebody else goes all the way around the board and lands on that space between Park Place and Boardwalk—Luxury Tax, $75. They put $75 in the middle of the board. When do you get to collect the money in the middle of the board? When you hit Free Parking, right?

Caught you! This isn't in the official rules of Monopoly.

As these examples illustrate, if you don't go over the ground rules before you start, there can be misunderstandings and disagreements. The same thing applies on your teams and in your business.

When I was working as a branch manager for a mortgage company, our processors were having problems with cross-contamination of files. As I mentioned earlier, it is the job of the loan processor to ensure the timely and accurate packaging of loans to be sent out to underwriters and then coordinate with the loan-closing department.

One day, after returning to my office, I noticed that my lead processor had nine or ten file jackets open. This was a potential challenge because data could be cross-contaminated and end up in the wrong file. This had happened numerous times before and was an issue. Computers were not connected then, and the only clouds were the ones floating by in the sky.

I was upset when I saw so many files open at one time. My operations manager heard me and came out of her office. We decided to sit down and have a meeting consisting of the operations manager, our five processors, and me. We had to come up with a new ground rule ensuring that this issue did not continue.

In the meeting, we learned that the reason so many files were often out at one time was the amount of phone calls a processor could be dealing with at one time. The appraiser for the Johnson refinance, the selling agent wanting an update on the Schroeder purchase, and so on.

In light of this information, we devised a ground rule that on Monday, Wednesday and Thursday mornings, between 9:00 A.M. and 11:00 A.M., there would be zero inbound phone calls allowed to processors. In addition, loan originators would not interact with their processors during those times. If they needed something, they would have to talk to the operations manager, Susan. She would talk to the processor if she felt it was necessary. Even I, as the manager, could not go to a processor directly. I could only go to Susan.

What happened was our:

* Customer satisfaction scores skyrocketed almost immediately
* Overall production increased significantly
* First time approvals soared
* Processor error ratios dropped drastically

All of this occurred because we simply established an effective ground rule. Is it possible that the ground rules in another mortgage company or another division could be different?

Absolutely. It is about what works for the team and has been established and agreed upon by them. Ground rules can easily vary from team to team inasmuch as the team's rules are congruent with those of the organization.

In the forming stage, every team needs to have ground rules. When a team is in the forming stage, even though the team may have written the ground rules, members need to be held accountable by each other as well as by a strong leader.

A powerful result from the forming stage is that a level of vulnerability trust begins to develop between everyone involved, and before a team can advance, it is essential that trust be in place.

Stage 2: Storming

In this stage, instead of asking questions, team members are simply making demands. "John's doing that. I think John should do this and Sally should do that." Have you ever heard this? And let's not forget, "In my last company, we. . . ." While information from another company could be helpful, in this stage, it may come across as demanding and somewhat condescending

A significant point about the storming phase is that sub-groups develop and petty conflict begins to occur.

Sub-groups can be smokers versus nonsmokers, management versus unions, etc. These sub-groups could be newer employees versus longevity or full-time employees versus part-time help or contractors. Basically, if you can think of a sub-group, it can develop.

Sub-groups are a natural subset of the overall team and typically develop on their own without any assistance. One constant is that sub-groups develop and fight over the pettiest of things, including something that may have occurred earlier or a minor squabble that has little or no relevance.

In the mortgage business, we used to have loan officers (many who were paid entirely on commission) say to loan closers, "Without me, you wouldn't have a job." In response, a loan closer might say, "Without me doing your back-end paperwork, you wouldn't get a paycheck." This represents sub-groups trying to protect their territory and push blame to another sub-group rather than trying to work together as one cohesive team. These types of conflicts serve no one, and ultimately, it is likely a customer that pays the price. This is not a good business practice.

In the storming stage, team members will begin to push back and test boundaries. The proverbial honeymoon phase (the forming stage) is over. If strong and consistent boundaries are not established, your team could stay in the storming stage for an extended period of time. There is often conflict during this stage, and a leader must be a little less authoritative and more participative. It is also crucial to let the team experience a healthy form of conflict—meaning conflict around ideas, not personal attacks. As we talked about earlier in my definition of an effective team, conflict around ideas is a healthy form of conflict and can only be accomplished once a significant level of trust has been established between everyone on the team.

Stage 3: Norming

Things begin to calm down in the norming stage. This is the point where you and other team members begin to recognize the purpose of the team, becoming less resistant to one another's ideas and change in general. Members essentially 'agree to disagree.' While team members may ask their leader questions, they are generally clarifying questions and not structure questions. Cooperation and collaboration increase significantly. It should be noted that as new projects and challenges face your team, there is a risk that you may slip back into the storming stage or possibly all the way back to forming. In the leader side, I will explain how this happens and how to prevent it. However, it is imperative that team members are also aware of what is happening within their own group.

Stage 4: Performing

Have you ever been on a team that just 'clicks'? When I ask that question in my workshops, I often have several people raise their hands. I try to find one who's in a management or leadership position and one who is a frontline employee.

I ask them both the same basic series of questions.

I will ask the manager, "How often did you see your team members?"

For the frontline, "How often did you see your manager?"

Sometimes I get the response, "Daily." I had one person tell me "quarterly" because he was a remote manager and his office was halfway across the country.

Even if their answer was that they met often, the manager was simply overseeing the team and letting the team run the course, not barking out orders to them. These managers are hands-off - answering questions, but available as needed.

Next, I would ask, "How busy were you during those times?"

Regardless of the position, the answer is often, "Very busy" to "Absolutely slammed."

I would follow that up with "How much work was there, on a one-to-ten scale?"

Many times, the answer is "seven" or higher.

I then ask, "On the same scale, how much stress was there?"

On average, I get a "9," or sometimes an "11."

My last question is, "On the one-to-ten scale, how much fun did you and the team have?"

Again, without hesitation and typically with a big smile on their face, I usually get a "9" or higher.

How is it possible to have a very high fun factor when the stress and workload are also high? In the performing stage, even though there may be higher stress and more work, the team members and manager are happier and much more productive than they are in other stages of team development. Inevitably, the fun factor is high, and when the fun factor is high, the team is more productive.

Extra Credit Stage: Adjourning

In 1977, Bruce Tuckman added another stage that some teams experience. Typically, this stage occurs when the team has been assembled for a specific project and the project is complete. It is time to disband. This is more common today, as we are constantly working on a variety of projects. This can also happen if there is restructuring within an organization. This can be a difficult time for some team members and leaders, as they may be unsure of their futures.

Teams are given a single project to accomplish and then they move on to another project or even another department. Having a sense of how to disband can leave the members with a better sense of accomplishment and sets up the next time the team members may be asked to work together.

✸ Which Stage Is Your Team In Right Now?

Try to determine which stage of matriculation your team is in. A competent leader should be able to provide you feedback to help you make this determination, as will be discussed in the leader side of the book. As I have mentioned, as a team member, it helps to know where you are to get a better sense of where you want to go.

* Is your team in the forming stage, asking a lot of questions?
* Is your team in the storming stage, making demands and bickering?
* Is your team in the norming stage and starting to think like a team, but really still not quite there? Are you agreeing but not quite totally?
* Or are you a high-performing team that just clicks on all cylinders?

☐ Forming   ☐ Norming
☐ Storming   ☐ Performing

Once you have identified what stage of the matriculation process your team is in, and assuming your team is not in the forming stage, it is critical to recognize that there are three things that can send your team all the way back to the forming stage.

* A change in leadership. This change can be at any level.
* A significant change in personnel. If you have a team of ten and you lose one, that's probably not going to send you back to forming, but if you lose four due to promotions or division splits, then you're looking at a significant change.

✳   A variation like a significant change in corporate direction.
     Possibly a merger or a takeover. Likewise, it could be the
     launch of a brand new business line.

When changes like these occur, they can disrupt, disband, or challenge a team. Having a strong core and sense of purpose can be the superglue to help the team's ship weather any storms they may encounter.

✳ Myths about Effective Teams

Now that you understand a bit more about what teams are, it's time to look at what they are not. Some of these may surprise you, but they will definitely give you pause for thought. There is just as much misinformation as there is information about what makes an effective team. I have assembled some of the top myths here. These myths can create a gap that can prevent team cohesion. Remember, the goal is to have everyone pointed in the same direction, knowing their roles, and committed to an outcome that benefits the whole team and, ultimately, the organization they are working for.

Myth 1: Teams are always self-directed

Teams are not automatically self-directed. Teams can become self-directed. Sometimes, teams are given their orders and have a defined purpose for a short amount of time. They have a task, they are given the parameters, and they get to work. Many committees are teams with a specific expected outcome. They are not necessarily self-directed, as they may take their orders externally. Another example is a jury. This is a short-term team. Even though they pick a foreman as a leader, they are often given a specific task and parameters by the judge, even though the judge has no part in the deliberations.

Myth 2: Work team participation can be mandated

Ever try to get a cat to play fetch? It is an exercise in futility. Here is a lesson for leaders - you cannot make anyone do anything they don't want to do. As a team member, a leader may ask you to do something, or insist that you do it, but we all have a choice. There may be reasons that you do not agree with a mandate, but as a team member, you must remember to handle each situation with respect. Sometimes, a team works best when members are allowed to work the way they work best. This may mean that they work from home part of the time. Some teams need a more hands-on approach, while others do better with a leader that supports rather than directs.

Myth 3: Employees want to always be empowered and to work as teams

Do you remember the first time you were asked to work in a group in school? What was that experience like? Were you a leader or just a member of the group? More importantly, what was the experience like for you? Some people just like to work alone and do not enjoy working on a team. They do not feel empowered by working on a team, and in some cases, they hate it. If there are a number of people on your team that don't enjoy working in a team environment, this could be disastrous. Later in this book, we will discuss how to assess the make-up of your team using the Everything DiSC model.

Myth 4: Every team decision requires a consensus

As we've discussed, the captain of the ship must make many of the decisions. In a team, some decisions may be left to the team members themselves. Some of these decisions do not require consensus. I doubt my father looked to the entire crew to decide what was going to be on the menu for dinner on the hospital ship. He may have asked other people in the kitchen, and they would go with a majority rules type of decision-making. Most of the time, someone in a group will not be happy with a particular decision, but that person still has a responsibility to support the team and respect the leadership.

Myth 5: Work teams are free or cheap

When was the last time anything worth having was free? A work team's value lies not in their salary, but in the product they produce.

Myth 6: Work teams always produce error-free work.

Here again is the adage about only being as strong as your weakest link. A poorly organized, unmotivated team will not produce anything but errors. It is vital to remember that teams are comprised of people and people will make mistakes. Great teams focus on what went wrong, not who messed up, and quickly move beyond the past to focus on the future. You cannot change the past; you can only alter your course for the future.

Myth 7: Work teams are new

The idea of a work team has existed since we were hunter-gatherers, but not exactly in the way it is used in companies today. The idea of teams can be traced back to the late 1920s. There was a series of studies called The Hawthorne Studies, in which workers were faced with different conditions. What the research showed was that work teams increased production and worker interaction. They found that the most significant factors in these teams were:

* A sense of group identity
* A feeling of social support
* Team cohesion

Elton Mayo, who was one of the researchers on The Hawthorne Studies, developed a list of factors that helped to create an effective work team. These factors are still relevant today:

* The manager (chief observer) had a personal interest in each person's achievements.
* The manager took pride in the record of the group.
* The manager helped the group work together to set its own conditions of work.
* The manager faithfully posted feedback on performance.
* The group took pride in its own achievements and had the satisfaction of outsiders showing interest in what they did.
* The group did not feel that they were being pressured to change.

   ✳   Before changes were made, the group was consulted.
   ✳   The group developed a sense of confidence and candor.

These research findings spurred companies to seriously consider the idea of grouping their employees into effective work teams, and to this day, they are still important considerations for human resource developers.[1]

✸   Team Player Thinking

Part of the anatomy of an effective team is the way they think and, ultimately, act on a daily basis. Here is a simple assessment tool to provide you with some insight about how your team thinks. Keep in mind that this is your opinion, and I encourage you to share this tool with others on your team and even your leader to see if you all view your team the same way.

     You may find areas in which you agree and some in which you do not. Talk about both to find consensus and ways to improve the score within your team. Remember: open conversation within the team is healthy — even if you disagree.

---

1. (Dyer, J. L., 1984. "Team research and team training: A state-of-the-art review." *Human Factors Review*, pp. 285-319.)

Consider each of the following statements separately. Place a circle around the number you feel best identifies the immediate team you work with on a regular basis. The scoring range is: 1 = least like your team and 5 = most like your team.

1. We look for ways to assist each other	1	2	3	4	5
2. We all respect each other's viewpoints	1	2	3	4	5
3. We ask for feedback from each other about our performance	1	2	3	4	5
4. We believe we can constantly improve our actions & performance	1	2	3	4	5
5. We look for ways to encourage each other	1	2	3	4	5
6. We review and eliminate old ways of doing things	1	2	3	4	5
7. We believe in taking control of our behavior and constantly moving in the direction of our mission	1	2	3	4	5
8. We accept and learn from our mistakes	1	2	3	4	5
9. We respect each other	1	2	3	4	5
10. We know something personal about each of our teammates — e.g., likes, dislikes, significant other, pet and children's names	1	2	3	4	5

TOTAL SCORE FOR CIRCLES_____

Results:

45-50: Congratulations - In your opinion, your team thinks like an effective team.

38-44: Your team may be experiencing some hiccups, but you can recover. There are likely one or two minor issues. Go back and see if there are any similarities in the lower scores. It may just be one type of situation or perhaps one person on the team that you feel is generating the problem. Either way, it can be easily managed.

37 or below: Your team needs some significant help. There are potentially several areas of concern. Be sure to look for patterns and determine what may be causing your team's discomfort. This could be from specific situations or projects. Research is your friend here.

You may download a PDF version of this assessment to print out and share with other members on your team. **http://bonuses.teamsrock. com**

You now have an idea of what an effective team looks like and thinks like as well as what stage your team may be in. All of this information is important as we begin to explore the behaviors of effective teams.

Chapter 3 Behaviors in an Effective Team

It is easy to draw a picture of what a perfect team may act like or perform like under the best of conditions. Let's face it, we are all human beings, and that means we are individuals with strengths and flaws. None of us thinks in the same way as everyone else, and therefore, our actions, beliefs and values may be different. Let me ask you a question that I frequently ask in my sessions. What would the world be like if everyone was exactly the same? Obviously, the answer is "boring." It is truly our differences that make us better and stronger, collectively. Each of us has a different style in which we operate, and the vast majority of the time, those differences make for a well-rounded team.

This chapter explores what different roles each individual team member may have and how to integrate and work well with others on the team. We all possess different skills, experiences, personalities, and perspectives. These differences should be placed on the table with other team members and utilized for the benefit of the entire team. Being different is not the same as being irrelevant. Just because someone may have a different perspective does not mean that there is not value in their perspective. On the contrary, it provides context and material for discussion. If everyone rubber-stamps ideas, then there can be no room for innovation or growth for the team.

While it may be the leader's job to facilitate dialogue and help the team assess ideas, in the end, it is up to individual team members to bring ideas forth to be considered. There is a certain amount of respect that has to be allotted when ideas or perspectives are presented. Again, ideas can be different — and different is not the same as wrong. Listen and really try to be empathetic to your teammate's experiences and views. This mindset not only benefits the team, but can also facilitate personal growth and development.

We begin this chapter with the idea that in order to be a good team member, you have to be a good follower. In order to be a valuable part of the team, you must be able and willing to listen to and follow the leader.

Followership

> *"If you act like an ass, don't get insulted if people ride you."*
>
> **– YIDDISH PROVERB**

Leadership styles have been talked about and dissected for decades, while the concept of being a valuable follower is somewhat new. Followership training brings connotations of negative thoughts because we try to breed leaders. Do followers do what they are told? Do they always say "Yes"?

Of course not. We are all followers to a certain level, and as followers, we need to be collaborators amongst ourselves as well as with our leaders, ultimately ensuring the success of the organizational mission and vision.

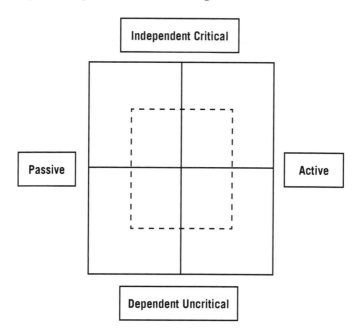

✸   What Type of Follower Are You?

The emergence of the concept of followership is attributed to professor at the Graduate School of Industrial Administration at Carnegie Mellon University and author, Robert Kelley.

According to Kelley, the concept of followership holds that team members should be viewed as collaborators, in sync with the team leader or management, to accomplish team and organizational goals.

Most followers fall into one of two broad categories: those who are independent critical thinkers and those who are dependent non-critical thinkers. The theory also suggests that while independent critical thinkers are preferred, the trait can be considered even more valuable when the follower is a creative problem solver. As you might imagine, those who are not self-motivated and take no initiative do not make good team members and will need constant supervision. Team members who need more or constant supervision limit what the team can accomplish, as they will tend to avoid responsibility for their contributions.

Kelley's concept goes on to further break down these traits into five subcategories. In the Leader side, we will review each of these subcategories in more detail.

1. Alienated followers (Independent-Passive)
2. Conformist followers (Dependent-Active)
3. Pragmatist followers (Doesn't fit into any of the barometers)
4. Passive followers (Dependent-Passive)
5. Exemplary followers (Independent-Active)

While leadership skills are most strongly promoted, good follow-ership skills are frequently underrated or considered undesirable by the leader as well as the follower. In this sense, climbing the corporate ladder can be more difficult if those on the next higher rung feel threatened in any way.

Some team members may feel intimidated by good followers. This is when terms like "brown-noser" may be heard. The paradox is that good leaders must emerge from great followers; those adept at utilizing followership skills to achieve personal goals without sacrificing the team's objectives will succeed.

Poor followership skills ultimately undermine the individual's leadership skills. Therefore, it is important to develop great followership skills; remember that as team members and followers, you are laying the path for the team's success. Here are a few skills that make good followers.

Good Judgment

While team members seek to follow the leader's directives, having a solid grasp of the organization's ethics and goals, as well as what it will take to achieve them, makes you a valuable follower. Great followers must know enough to respect decisions and yet be able to question them with problem-solving logic when appropriate.

Competence

Competence at assigned tasks is critical if they are to be done well. An excellent follower is always looking to improve his or her competency skills in order to make him or her more valuable to the leader and the team in general.

Honesty

No valid relationship can exist without honesty. This is all the more true between a follower and a team leader. Respect for position and experience is something to be valued, and true honesty even more so. A first-rate follower is unafraid to offer his or her comments. Honesty leads to integrity, and integrity leads to respect. Many define integrity as doing what you say you are going to do when you say you are going to do it, even when no one else is watching.

Courage

On the heels of honesty comes courage. Top-notch followers must have the courage to speak up and voice their honest feelings. This is not a false bravado for attention's sake. It is the courage of your convictions that allows you to say, "The emperor is not wearing clothes." (Hans Christian Andersen — "The Emperor's New Clothes")

Discretion

You have known that sinking feeling when you shared something very sensitive with another individual, and as soon as it was out of your mouth, you knew you had made a mistake. This is why the ability to be discreet is a valued commodity. Discretion makes you a good confidante, and being a good confidante proves your value to others and enhances vulnerability trust.

Loyalty

Loyalty to one's team and team leader is an expression of faith in their performance, judgment, and dedication to the goal. As a follower, this is critical when the waters become turbulent. There must be a high level of trust in place that allows you to navigate these rocky waters. Growing up, if you had several siblings, you more than likely fought among yourselves regularly, but when anyone from the outside picked on any one of you, you all banded together – that is loyalty.

Ego Management

There is little room for individual egos in a team situation; they fly in the face of the logic behind the concept of being a "team." A good follower understands this and reserves his ego for more appropriate situations.

During my time in mortgage banking, there was a problem that was affecting our office cohesion — egos were getting in the way of performance and it was affecting the overall morale of the team.

One Saturday, my wife and I were running errands and dropped in at a neighborhood yard sale. I found an old-fashioned coat tree, which gave me an idea. I purchased it and placed it in the office break room, because everyone stopped there before going to their desks, and this was a great place for them to hang their coats. I placed a sign above the coat tree that read:

> ## "Please Check Your Hats, Coats, and Egos Here."

This simple action delivered the desired effect and provided a little levity at the same time.

 Four Traits of Effective Team Members

Through my working with teams over the last 20 years, both in workshops and presentations, there are four traits that I have found to be consistent with effective team members. As we mentioned in the beginning of the chapter, none of us can be everything all the time. When we have an idea, or even a person, to model ourselves after, it makes the process of becoming effective team members much easier.

Trait 1: Effective team members learn to put the team before their own personal agendas.

In basketball, Dennis Rodman was considered by many to be an excellent defender. In his early years, he was not necessarily considered a great team player. When he got to Chicago and played under Phil Jackson with Michael Jordan and Scottie Pippen, everybody knew their role on the team and everyone on the team could achieve great things. As an individual, Dennis Rodman was very flamboyant and even made public appearances in a wedding dress. While on the court, however, he set aside his individuality and was all about the team.

In 2005, Jerry Colangelo became involved with USA Basketball. At that time, the team had not won a major international competition since 2000. He confidently rebuilt the program, gaining involvement from some of the NBA's top players as well as some highly respected coaches. One of his main focuses of the rebuilding process was making sure that the team's players were committed to the team. He knew that a cohesive team, one that played together on a regular basis, would be better than having players joining and leaving the team. He made each player commit to a three-year contract with the team when they signed on to demonstrate their commitment. From when he took over in 2005 through 2014, USA Basketball had a 75 — 1 record, amassing an astonishing .987 winning percentage, including gold medals at FIBA International competitions. Additionally, the team won Gold at the Beijing 2008 and London 2012 Olympics.

Trait 2: Effective team members are willing to volunteer for new assignments and tasks.

Today, the average person will work in seven different careers during a lifetime. They may have dozens of jobs within those careers. The days of working at one company like our fathers and grandfathers did and getting a gold watch after thirty or forty years are long gone. To make yourself and your team more valuable, it is beneficial to volunteer for new assignments. Remember, if you continually grow, your team will as well. By volunteering for more assignments, you make yourself more valuable to the team and yourself. This does not mean you should volunteer for every assignment. You must be conscientious about what you volunteer for. Remember, you don't want to burn yourself out.

Trait 3: Effective team members are willing to modify their views to reach a team consensus.

In order to gain commitment in the team, team members must be willing to modify their view, reach a team consensus, and achieve buy-in. Assume for a moment that you and Susan have worked together and built a strong level of vulnerability trust. During the process of working together, you and Susan have had differing opinions about how to do some things. It is important that you both feel your voices are heard and that everybody has listened. After you have both shared your views, and the team goes with your approach, then it is easy for Susan to buy in and be willing to modify her view.

On the other hand, if you had not had conflict around ideas but had just started bantering, and your view was accepted and Susan's was not, she may conform; however, because she did not truly buy in, she may subconsciously sabotage the project.

I once attended a meeting for a local association. One of the things on the agenda was whether to give the board the ability to raise dues for our membership from two percent a year to five percent a year.

Going into the meeting, I was opposed to the idea. "No, I don't like that," I said. "I don't have a problem if we need the five percent, but I do have a problem giving the board "carte blanche," the ability to raise those dues."

In an open discussion, we had some very good conversation. While I was not a hundred percent in favor of it, I understood where they were coming from, and I felt my concern was heard. The vote passed, and because I felt that my voice was heard, I supported their decision 100%.

Trait 4: Effective team members are open to new ideas for the benefit of the ultimate team.

How many workplaces today have people who have great ideas?

All of them, right?

In some places, team members are afraid to offer their ideas because they're concerned they are going to be shot down by someone else. To ensure that the team is effective, everybody has to be open to new ways of doing things. Steve Jobs was brilliant at getting us to buy things we didn't know we needed. You've got to be open to new ideas because they will often help the whole team.

You cannot be a team member with blinders on. It is not enough to sit in your office or cubicle with your head down and expect to be an effective team member. You must be aware of both what is going on around you and the people around you. For more intro-verted individuals, this can be a little intimidating, but with some practice and trust, anyone can come out of their shell and be an active member of a team.

The more acutely aware you are of a situation, the more effective you can, and will, be. Think about it like this: have you ever been driving on the interstate with your exit coming up a mile or so away on a multi-lane highway? You carefully merge over to the right lane to take the exit. As you're getting over to that right lane, just before you move to the exit lane, a car flies up from behind you, zips around you on the left, stares at you with a dirty look, then cuts back in front of you and takes a nose dive down the same exit ramp you are taking.

Has that ever happened to you?

Now imagine that at the end of the ramp, there's a traffic signal — about 70% of the time, it is what color?

Red, right? You pull up to that traffic signal right next to that guy who just gave you a dirty look. You look over at him and smile. Whose blood pressure is higher? This is what I like to call 'Hood Ornament Syndrome.' Simply put, it is where the other person can only see as far as the hood ornament on their car.

I can remember the first time I ever heard my grandmother use the phrase, "Hurry up and wait." I was about ten years old and I was in the back seat of the car. My mom was driving and my grandmother was in the front passenger seat. We were just driving down the road and could easily see the red light up ahead when a car flew right by us and locked on its breaks. That's when my grandmother said "Hurry up and wait," as we pulled up next to them.

Is that how you're running your life today? Is that how your team operates? Are they planning, are they focusing, are they looking at things? Are they always putting out fires or are they planning?

You have to be aware of what is going on around you. There is a term for this: Awareness Brings Effectiveness, or **ABE**, as I like to refer to it.

✸ Awareness Brings Effectiveness — The ABE Effect

When we are aware of what is going on around us, we can often resolve situations before they start to become issues. We are also aware of upcoming deadlines, new projects, and events that directly impact us, both individually and as a team. We are ahead of the curve ball, not just swinging at the last minute and missing.

Have you ever watched somebody who was so focused on one thing that they had zero comprehension of what was going on around them?

Here is an exercise to illustrate this idea. If you would like to try it, you will need to read the next selection first and find a willing partner. You will be leading the exercise to help your partner have a visual understanding of ABE.

✳ Awareness Exercise

Make sure your partner's hands are free. Ask them to take their right hand, extend it straight out in front of them, with their fingers pointing up and the palm open and facing them.

Have them close their fingers and ask them to focus on the little space between their two middle fingers. With their arm still extended, have them take that arm and move it all the way to their far right, then all the way to their far left, then all the way back to their far right. Have them do this five or six times really fast, all the time focusing on the gap in their fingers.

While they are doing this, you stand in front of them about six feet away and flash three sets of numbers at them with your fingers, in random order. This should take no more than one or two minutes.

After you complete this exercise, ask them to tell you the numbers you flashed. Can they recall all of them? How about one or two of them? More than likely, if they were concentrating on their fingers, they could not see the numbers that you flashed in front of them. They were so focused on the gap between their fingers that they were unaware of what was going on around them. When you are on a team, you have to be aware of what you are doing as well as what others are doing around you. This is the basis of ABE, and it benefits both you and your team.

The concept of ABE brings up another subject that is very essential, one that we explored a bit in followership - and that is personal responsibility. Knowing your position on a team is important and so is taking responsibility for dropping the ball from time to time. Let's face it — WE HAVE ALL DONE IT! We will all do it again at some point. It happens to every one of us. We are humans, not machines (although there can be computer errors too). The thing we all try to avoid is making too many mistakes or repeating the same mistakes. If you practice ABE and the other concepts here, you will definitely reduce mistakes and errors. It is more important to take ownership and focus on solutions than to dwell on the fact that you made a mistake.

> *"It is not whether you get knocked down;*
> *it is about how fast you get back up."*
>
> **—GREGG GREGORY**

How do you get back up? Many times, you have to take the seat of your OWN pants and pull yourself back up.

10 Little Words…

There are ten little words that have had a significant impact on my life, even though it has been over forty years since I originally heard them. I share those words and this story to wrap up this chapter because they can be life-changing. If you use these 10 little words, you will always come back to the path of being an effective team member.

It was September 1973, and I was a junior in high school. From 1954-1994, High Point High School in Beltsville, Maryland only had two principals. Frank Tracy took over in the fall of 1973. He wanted to leave his mark early on. I remember that it was a hot September afternoon when he held his first assembly in the gym.

My high school graduating class had 751 students, and the classes before and after us had about the same. This meant that in this assembly, we had over 2,000 people including teachers, administrators, and staff in the gym this hot September afternoon.

As Mr. Tracy began to speak, I noticed that he was speaking to the students and not at the students. Somewhere in his speech, he paused and said, "Ladies and gentlemen, I want to share with you the secret to success. The secret to success is really quite simple, and it comes in just 10 little words. Like the Gettysburg address delivered by President Lincoln in 1863, these are all simple words. In fact, each word has just one syllable and two letters. It is when you string these 10 little words in this particular order that they become the secret to your success. I don't mean just your success at High Point High School; I mean your success throughout life."

Now let's be clear - I was a junior in high school, so was I really listening to what he was saying? What was more important? Girls, cars, sports, and food were much more important. The day of the week and time of day would actually determine what was more important at any given time.

I did not realize I was actually living the words until almost 20 years after I graduated from high school. Somewhere along the line, I realized that I had never had a job where I relied on a salary to pay my bills. Every job in my adult life has been either 100% commission or my own company. As a manager, I received a small salary with the bulk of my income coming from the production of others on the team.

After I came to this realization, I began to practice living the words on a regular basis. I even purchased a card with the 10 little words on it and sent it to Mr. Tracy.

High Point High School is located in the metropolitan area of Washington, DC, and I had the pleasure of speaking there a few years ago. In several of my workshops, I have had High Point graduates in attendance, and as I begin this story, they look at their neighbor in the class and say, "I know the words." That is the impact that Mr. Tracy had on everyone he met.

At the opening day of the 1999 Baltimore Orioles baseball season, I was taking a walk around Oriole Park at Camden Yards when I noticed a man coming toward me. As I looked closer, I realized that it was Mr. Tracy. I stopped him and said, "Good morning, Mr. Tracy. How are you?" He responded, "Good morning, Mr. Gregory. I am wonderful and how are you?" It had been almost 24 years since I had graduated, and he still remembered my name.

I can truly say that these 10 little words have been the personal focus of my life, both personally and professionally. I guess you could say they have been the track I have been running on for years, and

I would like to continue the Frank Tracy tradition and share them with you now. Please write them down and read them every day in the morning before you begin your day. Remember, there are just two letters for each word.

> ## If it is to be,
> ## it is up to me

It is not up to your mother, your father, your brother, your sister, your aunt or uncle, your cousin, your friends, your company, your boss, or even your co-worker. It is up to you and only you.

As a footnote to this story, Mr. Tracy passed away in 2015. When I went to the funeral home viewing on a Sunday afternoon, I was one of over 300 people who attended, including students from every year he was principal and teachers I had not seen since I graduated 40 years earlier. Many of these teachers told me he was the best principal they had ever worked for.

Chapter 4 Communicating Effectively

Effective communication skills are the building blocks to every aspect of life, and they are especially critical in teamwork. A cohesive team simply cannot exist without them. In this chapter, we are going to explore some strategies and shortcuts for communicating more effectively with your teammates, including your team leader. These strategies can also be effective with customers and vendors. In short, these strategies work with virtually everyone you come in contact and do business with.

 Everything DiSC®

> *"The profiling tool I use is the Myers-Briggs Type Indicator.*
> *However, a number of other personality profiles are also popular*
> *and one of the best and most common is Everything DiSC."*
>
> —PATRICK M. LENCIONI, IN *THE FIVE DYSFUNCTIONS OF A TEAM,*
>
> *ENHANCED EDITION: A LEADERSHIP FABLE*

Wouldn't it be great if you knew how to decode a teammate's message based upon his or her behavior style? Would it help to know the best way to work with colleagues, your manager, and even clients based upon how your personality interacts with theirs?

One of the most powerful tools I utilize with my clients and recommend to others is Everything DiSC. This tool allows you to determine your behavior style and provides insight on how to communicate and work with other behavior styles. If you know the

Everything DiSC profile of someone else, it can really help you to save time and avoid unnecessary conflict

Wiley, the company that provides the Everything DiSC assessment, offers a number of different Everything DiSC evaluation profiles, and each provides you with different information.

The evaluation provides insights into your dominant personality style. There is an area in which your particular dominant style falls — either 'D,' 'i,' 'S,' or 'C.'

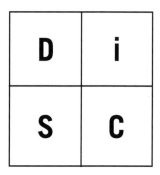

D (upper left quadrant) stands for dominance. Typically, these folks are:

* ✳ Interested in and focused on the bottom line or end results
* ✳ Task-driven
* ✳ Fast-paced
* ✳ Quicker decision makers

The way to work with them is get in and get out of conversations quickly, giving them pertinent information without overloading them with details, niceties, and social things. The approach referred to as "The 3 Be's" works well here:

* ✳ Be Brief
* ✳ Be Direct
* ✳ Be Gone

i (upper right quadrant) stands for influence. These people are:

 ✳ Fast-paced like the D
 ✳ More of social butterflies
 ✳ More enthusiastic
 ✳ Relatively quick decision makers

S (lower right quadrant) stands for Steadiness. These people are:

 ✳ Very structured in what they do
 ✳ Likely to take their time
 ✳ Fond of thinking things through from a variety of angles
 ✳ Likely to process things a little differently. Not wrong,
    just differently.
 ✳ Happier when everyone is getting along

Now, because they are diametrically opposite of the D, the two can sometimes have challenges because they value things differently. The D would be somebody who works at a faster pace, wanting quick decisions. The S is slower paced, is slower to make decisions, and thinks through things. So sometimes when they're working together, they may frustrate each other.

C (lower left quadrant) stands for Conscientiousness. These people are:

 ✳ Very conscientious about their work
 ✳ Focused on quality of the work
 ✳ Very detail-oriented
 ✳ Likely to take their time and focus on accuracy
 ✳ Likely to think things through with an analytical approach

It is important to understand that we are all a blend of all four styles.
     Once everyone on a team knows their natural style, I suggest they put up a little card with the quadrant and their dot on their cubicle or office to remind others what their go-to style is. In addition, write down three things that will help others work with you better. You will be able to draw these from your personalized Everything DiSC profile report, which is about 20 pages long.

My dominant style is "D", so I would write:

"To work with me better you should:

* Speak directly,
* Be upfront,
* Don't be offended if I'm direct."

Once you understand your profile and how Everything DiSC works, you can begin to understand and read other people more accurately. You can never be sure of another person's style unless they tell you, but you can use Everything DiSC as a way to understand their needs.

It is critical to understand that there are no good or bad styles and that all styles have strengths and limitations.

In order to understand what a person is trying to say or is feeling, you should consider the other ways people communicate beyond the words coming out of their mouth:

* Body language such as posture, use of hands, and facial expressions
* Tone of voice and expressions such as pace, inflection, and volume

To further explore the idea that effective communication goes beyond just the spoken, or even written, word, I offer the Three V's of communication.

⊛ The Three V's

The Three V's represent the different ways in which we communicate with one another.

* Verbal (the words we use)
* Vocal (tonality of the words)
* Visual (seeing the person speak)

We use each of these three V's in every communication, in different proportions.

1: Verbal

Verbal is the way most of us think about communicating. It is simply the words we choose. Some words can inspire cooperation, while other words can be what some might call "fightin' words." The words we use are very, very important. The greatest mistake people make is speaking or hitting "send" before they really consider the words they are choosing to communicate. Taking a pause before we speak or write can save us loads of regret and backtracking. We can express what we are feeling with words without using them as weapons.

2: Vocal

Vocal is about how we use the tonality of our voices. There are three parts of vocal communication that I refer to as the three P's:

* Pitch
* Power
* Pace

Pitch is the level of inflection that's used, going from way up (think Tweety Bird) to way down (think Darth Vader). Power is how loudly or softly, or the volume at which we are talking. Pace refers to how quickly or slowly you are speaking. The average person speaks about 110-130 words per minute, but professional speakers speak closer to 150-160 words per minute, and auctioneers are in the 250 wpm range. I tend to be a fast talker. I typically speak at a rate of 160 WPM and sometimes I have gusts upwards to 300 WPM.

3: Visual

The visual component is your eye contact, body language and other nonverbal vocal skills, such as the way you use your hand gestures and things of that nature.

While the visual component is partially influenced by the way people dress, that is only part of the equation. In my workshops, I'll sometimes do something where I'll say, "Imagine that instead of coming in business or business casual attire, I had a pair of jeans that were ripped at both knees and two sizes too big, and I was wearing a tie-dyed t-shirt. Imagine my hair was long and pulled into a ponytail, and from its appearance, it had not been washed in a day or two. In addition, I am sporting an earring, lip ring, nose ring, brow ring, and maybe a few other rings that we won't discuss. Imagine that I haven't shaved in three or four days. I have a tattoo of a giant dragon's tail that starts on the back of my neck and goes down my right arm."

I then ask participants how they would feel if I came in dressed like this, and about 70-80% of the people say, "I'm out of here." A smaller percentage of people say that they would listen for a little bit and make a decision later. Then a very microscopic percentage says that I must be good in order for their company or organization to bring me in looking like that.

In order to demonstrate how visual information can affect communication and even perception, I will illustrate it with a story about a big man with tattoos.

✦ Don't Judge a Wrestler by his Tattoos

A number of years ago, I met a professional wrestler, Prince Albert (Matt Bloom is a world champion who also went under the moniker of Albert, A-Train, Lord Tensai, Sweet T, and Giant Bernard.)

When I met him, I originally had no idea who he was or what he did. I ran into him on a rental car bus at LAX one day. He is a huge man covered in tattoos; he has multiple piercings and appeared to be pushing 400 pounds. Without knowing him or what he did, my initial thought, looking at him with his tattoos and piercings, was, "Okay, this guy is a little crazy." I tried hard not to stare or act like I was paying attention to him. After a couple of minutes, I overheard him on his cell phone sounding like a Wall Street executive. Because he was so professionally spoken, I could imagine him wearing a suit and working for a Fortune 500 company. When we got off the bus, I said something to him. He turned around and we started to talk and had the most enjoyable conversation. I told him that I teach people about communication and mentioned how impressed I was by his demeanor and how it made him appear professional, confident, and like someone to be respected.

He thanked me for recognizing that, but admitted that many people don't get past the visual part. He said he had a master's degree in education. He taught at a deaf school for a number of years before becoming a professional wrestler. I thought that was really fascinating, and thought about how we judge the book by the cover. In communication with our teams, our colleagues, and our customers, we often have to be very careful about that.

There is another example from my own childhood about how someone judged me because of what I looked like, and my age. Sometimes we make the mistake of profiling people in the wrong way. As we discussed in the section about Everything DiSC, it is tough to evaluate someone just by looking at them, but we do it every day. It is important that we withhold judgment, listen, and ask questions first, or we can lose our teammate's respect or even a potential sale.

The United States Powerboat Show

When I was 17 years old, my father decided that he wanted to go to the US Powerboat show in Annapolis, Maryland. This boat show is the largest "in the water" power boat show in America. In fact, I have not missed a boat show since this show in 1975.

I was a typical 17-year-old kid with scraggly hair. It was a very nice day and I remember wearing a pair of denim shorts and a t-shirt. I was excited to be there and see all the boats, so I told my folks I was going to take off and look around. My father told me he was looking for a particular boat manufacturer.

The manufacturer he was looking for was Jersey Boat Works. The boat was a 40-foot Jersey sport fishing motor yacht. I wandered around and finally found it. Imagine, here is this kid that looks like Shaggy from *Scooby-Doo* getting on this very nice boat. As a salesperson, would you have talked to me?

I jumped on, looked around, and was exploring because I had heard a lot about this boat from my father. I went into the engine area and looked all around the yacht, and yet nobody would come talk to me. Not one sales person even looked at me, much less approached or talked with me.

Finally, Fred came onboard and started asking me some questions. I started asking him questions about the boat and we had a wonderful conversation, probably about 40 minutes.

I told Fred I had to go get my father, and when we came back, Fred started talking to Dad — and that is when we found out that Fred was not a salesperson. He was Fred H. McCarthy, the founder, owner, and CEO of Jersey Boat Works Incorporated.

I continued to go to the boat show for the next 17 years, and Fred made sure he told the story about meeting a 17-year-old kid to his salespeople. Over the years, he emphasized never ignoring anyone because my dad ended up buying the boat. Was I the decision maker? Not a chance. I was 17, but while I had no money, I was a huge influence with my father. That is key. Fred told that story to everyone. In 1992, Fred sold the Jersey Boat Works and introduced me to Bill and John Dalton, the two brothers who had just purchased the company. He said to them, "Do you remember last night at dinner, I was telling you about a kid that came to the show and that you cannot ignore anyone? Well, here is that kid."

Even though much of what we communicate when we are face-to-face with someone is visual, it is always smart not to judge the book by the proverbial cover. We should be observing behaviors and commonalities, and really assessing these things before we make a decision about someone.

Imagine that in your office, a colleague walks by and says nonchalantly, in a monotone voice, "Thanks for your help" without even making eye contact. How would you feel? Now imagine the same person walks by and goes out of their way to use your name and say how much they appreciated your help on something and thanks you for your support. Do you feel any differently this time?

The first time, they may have used the right words. The challenge was that they did not make eye contact and had virtually no voice inflection. This would typically lead you to disbelieve their sincerity.

In the second example, because they took extra time, made

strong eye contact, and used your name, they made you feel as if you were special. Have you ever had a conversation with someone who, even in a large room, makes you feel as though you are the only person in the room? This is a special person.

What is important to note is that your vocal and visual communication is actually more important than the words coming out of your mouth, as these two areas speak volumes about your mood and intention.

Communication by Phone

Technology has changed, and the way we communicate by phone has become so sophisticated that we can make video calls anywhere in the world. The way we communicate in those instances is the same as we would face-to-face. For those using the old-school way of using only audio, the 3 V's proportions change -the vocal becomes the dominant factor in communicating and how the person perceives what the sender is saying. Remember, this is about how the recipient feels when they hear your communication rather than the factual basis of the communication.

E.T.R.D.

Now, we are relying on the vocal cues from the person on the other end of the line. Read the following sentences aloud and make an emphasis on the italicized word. Listen to see if you get a different meaning or context in each sentence.

I did not say he let the dogs out.

I *did **not*** say he let the dogs out.

I did not ***say*** he let the dogs out.

I did not say ***he*** let the dogs out.

I did not say he ***let*** the dogs out.

I did not say he let the ***dog***s out.

I did not say he let the dogs ***out***.

Does the meaning change with each iteration of the sentence? While the words were the same, the meaning changed with our vocal inflection. This happens all the time in conversations. Try this exercise with a partner and ask them their opinion about the inflection and the meaning they glean from the sentence.

If you want to have some fun with this – do this exercise in a team meeting, and see how your team infers the communication

Communication occurs with two people. Even in group situations, the communication is between two people: the person sending the message and the person receiving it. How many times have you felt as if you were clear in what you were saying, and the other person completely misheard or interpreted it differently? How many lyrics have you sung for 20 years, only to find out what you thought were the right words were not even close?

It has been said that over 90% of all messages have a hidden message embedded to some degree. This includes messages that are spoken as well as the written word. To better understand these messages and how they are embedded, let's look at how the communication process works.

I use the following model to explain communication:

E- Encode
T- Transmit
R- Receive
D- Decode

Encoding occurs when you are communicating whether face-to-face, over the phone, in a voice mail message, or even using IM, texting, or email. Regardless of how you are communicating, you are trying to relay and transmit a message. The person (or persons) you are communicating with receives the message and then decodes your message. Successful communication occurs when your *encoded* message and their *decoded* message match exactly. As a child, you may have played the telephone game (sometimes called Whisper) with a circle of friends. You whisper a phrase into the person's ear on your right, and that person then repeats the message as a whisper into the person's ear on his or her right. This continues quickly around the circle until the person on your left whispers the message back into your ear. How distorted is the message by the time it gets back to you? More often than not, the message has changed into something very different and perhaps a bit silly, whether intentionally or because the person misheard it. This is a great example of encoding and decoding not being in alignment. It is all fun and games when you are in grade school, and it can create problems in the workplace.

It is so important, as the transmitter of information, that you are clear and that you make sure the receiver decoded your message correctly. As the receiver, you can rephrase what you just heard for clarification. Clarification is the key, because without it, you can never be sure that the person you are communicating with clearly understood the message you were trying to get across. As the recipient, you can use a technique called reflective listening, which is simply rephrasing the statement from another. While this is about 99.5% successful, there is a microscopic flaw when you stop here. To ensure that you are 100% correct in your understanding with reflective listening, after rephrasing the statement back — tag on a closed-ended question like, "Is this correct?" If you do not add the last question, in some cases, the person you are communicating with may not correct your understanding if you are wrong. By asking this closed-ended question, you ensure clarity.

For instance, if a person says, "Reports need to be in the box at 4:00 p.m., but no later than 4:15." This may need some reflective feedback.

"What I am hearing you say is that you prefer the reports to be in the box by 4:00, but you will continue to accept them as being on time until 4:15. Is that correct?"

Communication is important in day-to-day communications with our teammates. But what about communicating with our bosses? It is important that clear lines of communication exist between you and your leader, as this builds both understanding and trust.

It is important, as an employee, that you can communicate your accomplishments clearly. We cannot rely on our boss's memory of events that took place months ago any more than we can rely on our own memories. Yet, for many employees, that is what occurs at annual reviews.

One of the best ways to communicate something important is to write it down first. Then you not only have a record, but you have something to refer to other than your memory. A great way to ensure that you are communicating your accomplishments for the year is an accomplishments log.

✳ Accomplishments Log

For many people (employees and managers alike), having to go through multiple root canals sounds more appealing than going through the process of employee evaluations. One of the biggest issues for many people is that when they do the evaluation, both the manager and the employee can only clearly remember bigger circumstances and what has happened within the previous few weeks. You are stretching to remember what has happened over the past year, especially the good things.

Do you remember what you ate last night? How about last week? Most people can't remember, so writing it down can ensure that you know all of your accomplishments for the past year. When you do something, write down what you did, when you did it, and what impact it had on the team, project, or company. By the time you are ready for your evaluation, you are prepared, and frankly, if you give a copy to your manager before the evaluation process begins, it can be really helpful for your manager as well, because they are not required to remember everything either.

Another major benefit of keeping an accomplishments log is that when you are considering making a move to another team or department, you have a current list of everything you have done – not the things you were responsible for.

The dark stepsibling of effective communication is conflict, as it is inevitable that you will have to deal with conflict during your employment. Where there are two or more people involved, a potential conflict will arise at some point. Let's be clear – conflict around ideas is helpful, and conflict that involves personal attacks is poison.

Clear communication is essential during times of conflict. In the next chapter, we present strategies for not only how to handle conflict when it arises, but also how you might avoid it.

Chapter 5 Working Through Conflict with a Teammate

As we have talked about previously, having effective conflict around ideas is a very healthy way to grow, both individually and as a team. Have you ever been on a team where you were in a project meeting and nobody challenged or disagreed with anybody? What happens when that meeting is over and everyone goes back to their desks? Gossip and personal attacks behind everyone's back.

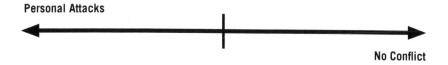

Personal Attacks

No Conflict

Imagine the line above as a continuum. On the far left is the extreme representing personal attacks, and on the far right is the extreme with no conflict. The line in the middle represents the halfway point between the two extremes. When there are no challenges among team members, the team is on the far right of the continuum, and there is absolutely no conflict. If, in a staff meeting, insults are flying and arguments are occurring, this represents the far left of the continuum. We know that personal attacks do not work either. So where is the best place to be? No conflict or war zone?

When I was 16 and taking my driver's license test, for some reason, there was one question I will never forget.

"When a vehicle is traveling on a two-way street and making a left hand turn onto a two-way street, where should the vehicle be placed?"

There were four answers, and while I do not remember the incorrect answers, I do remember the correct one: "To the right of and as close to the center line as possible."

Guess where conflict needs to be on your team? To the right of and as close to the center line as possible. You should avoid crossing that middle line into personal attack territory, while still getting your point across.

Having conflict around ideas is what we should strive for, and crossing that line is where team damage is done and trust begins eroding.

It is important to understand how conflict works as well as how to handle the stages to create the best possible outcome for everyone. Many personal conflicts can be avoided in the early stages through clear communication, respect, and reflective listening.

Three Stages of Conflict

Stage 1

During this stage, team members probably won't give enough information for you to truly determine their level of frustration. They will typically roll with the punches and reluctantly agree without much emotion. You may struggle to notice because the event that occurred is really a non-event for you. The challenge is that if the group does not make them comfortable, they may become slightly upset and then you may notice a slight increase in their breathing and sighing.

Stage 2

These folks are annoyed and exhibit mild irritation. You may notice frustrated sighs and rolling of the eyes. These team members' speech will become short and the inflection in their voices will drop at the end of a sentence. A common phrase you may hear is "Whatever!" At this stage, because you have failed to meet their expectations, you may notice an aura of negativity around them. It is important to recognize and acknowledge the team members at this point; otherwise, they will likely quickly escalate to Stage 3.

Stage 3

It is important to recognize that some people do not escalate to this stage; they actually start here, and that can be a huge challenge.

At this point, major feelings and frustrations are on full display. Increased volume is almost guaranteed, and profanity may be used. They feel like victims and are truly hurt by the lack of empathy, the way they are being treated, or the lack of service provided to them. These folks are quite easy to recognize and are likely noticed by everyone in the immediate area. I am sure you know the type.

There are strategies for handling conflict at each of these stages that can help prevent them from escalating while at the same time helping to resolve them. At every stage, you must keep your voice levels in control. It is important not to raise your volume. When you raise your volume, they will in turn raise theirs, and you may raise yours even further. Let's face it: no one wins at that point.

On the flip side, if you lower your voice, you acquiesce, and the other person will try to take advantage of that. Of course, that does not work either. You must maintain a confident and firm voice at the same level. Because emotions tend to take over, this is very easy to say and typically very difficult to enact.

Here are some strategies to help with each stage.

For Stage 1:

* Show surprise (not sarcasm) that the problem or incident occurred and be empathetic to the situation. Be sure to let the other person know that you take the issue seriously.
* Use normal communication and warm people skills – remain calm and collected. Engage them with questions.
* Show concern for them in a personal way. Thank them for understanding.
* Let them know that you are available to talk about the situation anytime.

For Stage 2:

- ＊ Display a sense of urgency, yet remain calm and collected.
- ＊ Involve the team member in the solution process, if possible.
- ＊ Provide added value and be helpful.
- ＊ Thank them for their patience and understanding.
- ＊ Sometimes admitting you were wrong, even if you were not, goes a long way.

For Stage 3:

- ＊ Allow the team member to vent.
- ＊ Be very empathetic and remain calm and collective.
- ＊ Describe their behavior if necessary – DO NOT tell them to calm down.
- ＊ Clarify by using reflective listening skills.
- ＊ Provide added value respective to the level of the problem.

One key strategy in each stage is involving the other person in solving the challenge. By utilizing this simple technique, you will experience a greater degree of success, as the person will truly buy into the solution. After all, it was, at least in part, their idea.

Years ago, I was working with a small team of about twelve people. We were going to produce an event for a weekend in Atlanta. It was late Friday night when we arrived, and we were all exhausted when checking into the hotel. As we were unloading our luggage from the hotel shuttle bus, I walked in to let the front desk know that we had arrived and that there was a large group of people checking in, while the executive director of the team stayed back with everyone else. The rooms were all supposed to be set up to be directly billed to the master account, while incidentals were going to be on individual credit cards. The front desk agent told me that the hotel sales team had not communicated this to them. I knew a problem was quickly developing.

I told them that the executive director was going to be coming in, that he was not going to be happy, and that he would probably go ballistic rather quickly. I asked the manager, "Is there anything we can do to handle this?"

"Sorry, my hands are tied until the morning," was the response I received.

As I walked back out to meet the rest of our team, I made a motion with the circle of my hands and pointed in the other direction. Everybody stopped and we let our executive director walk to the front desk.

I said to my team members, "Blowup about to occur in 5, 4, 3, 2, 1..."

"What the...!" echoed from across the lobby.

He was at a level three, and the best way to handle it was to allow him to vent. I'll give the front desk clerk and manager credit. They allowed him to vent. They both maintained their composure and eventually came up with a way to solve the problem. We all know that there were better ways to handle the situation from the executive director's view and, right or wrong, we all know people who simply start out at level three.

That same weekend, the executive director began yelling at me. He went off at me in public, venting, ranting, and raving. I had admittedly made a mistake, and we fixed it. As he and I walked through the hotel lobby, he was yelling at me, and he continued the yelling on the elevator all the way up to the suite.

At any point, I could have easily yelled back — especially while in public — and yet I simply let him continue to vent. When we got upstairs to the staff suite, I described the behavior to him in a confident and articulate voice. I clarified by using reflective listening and then I boldly stepped up and told him not to continue to speak to me in that tone of voice. I never told him to calm down. Remember, you cannot tell somebody to calm down. The two key things to do in those extreme situations are to allow the person to vent and describe the behavior.

Conflict is something that we all approach differently. We all have a vast array of experiences, and this can dictate how we cope. Whether dealing with colleagues, customers, or managers, it is critical to know how to respond in conflict situations.

Conflict Management Style Survey

Each of the following ten statements has five possible responses. Place the number 5 next to the best response for you. Next, place a 4 beside the next best response for you, followed by a 3 for the next best response for you. DO NOT rank numbers 1 or 2. Go through all 10 statements, in order, and do not skip questions. Do not agonize over your responses; your initial response is your most accurate.

For a copy of this assessment and other tools, go to **http:// bonuses. teamsrock.com**

1. When you see conflict emerging within your team, you would:

____ A: Push for a quick decision to ensure that the project or task is completed

____ B: Avoid outright confrontation by moving the discussion toward middle ground

____ C: Share with the team your impression of what is going on so that the nature of the conflict can be discussed

____ D: Ease the tension with humor

____ E: Stay out of the conflict as long as it does not concern you

2. When you have authority in a conflict solution, you would:

____ A: Put it straight and let everyone know your view

____ B: Try to negotiate the best settlement

____ C: Ask for the viewpoints of others and attempt to find a solution that both sides might try

____ D: Go along with others, providing support when and where you can

____ E: Tell those involved to resolve the conflict on their own

3. When you have strong opinions or feelings in a conflict situation, you would:

_____ A: Enjoy the emotional release and sense of exhilaration and accomplishment

_____ B: Enjoy the challenge of the conflict

_____ C: Become serious and concerned about how others are feeling and thinking

_____ D: Find it frightening and be concerned that someone will be hurt

_____ E: Become convinced that there is nothing you can do to resolve the issue

4. When disagreeing and becoming angry with others, you:

_____ A: Blow up without thinking about it

_____ B: Smooth things over with a good story

_____ C: Express your anger and welcome a response

_____ D: Compensate for your anger by acting the opposite of your feelings

_____ E: Remove yourself from the situation altogether

5. When someone takes an illogical position, you:

_____ A: Tell them you don't like it

_____ B: Casually let them know you're not happy; distract with humor to avoid confrontation

_____ C: Draw out the conflict and explore mutually acceptable solutions

_____ D: Say nothing and keep your feelings to yourself

_____ E: Allow your actions to speak for you

6. When someone on the team opposes the rest of the group, you would:

_____ A: Publicly point out that this person is hindering the group and suggest that everyone move forward without him or her

_____ B: Ensure that this person has an opportunity to communicate his or her objections so a compromise can be reached

_____ C: Attempt to uncover why this person views the issue differently, allowing the group to re-evaluate the issue

_____ D: Encourage everyone to set aside the conflict and move on to friendlier items

_____ E: Remain silent and avoid getting involved

7. What is the best result you can expect from conflict?

_____ A: It helps everyone face the facts

_____ B: Conflict will counterbalance extreme views in thinking, so a strong middle ground can be accomplished

_____ C: Conflict clears the air and boosts commitment and results

_____ D: It illustrates how absurd self-centeredness is and draws everyone closer

_____ E: It minimizes the complacency and assigns blame where it belongs

8. When you disagree with other team members on a project, you:

_____ A: Stand by your beliefs and define your point of view to everyone

_____ B: Appeal to the logic of everyone, and hope to convince a majority you're right

_____ C: Explore various points of agreement and disagreement with everyone, then seek alternatives that include all viewpoints

_____ D: Simply go along with the group

_____ E: Don't participate in the discussion or feel bound by any decision they reach

9. In your opinion, the primary reason for groups not working with each other is:

_____ A: Lack of a clearly stated position or failure to back up the team's position

_____ B: A tendency of the team to force leaders to agree with the decision, as opposed to encouraging flexibility leading to a compromise

_____ C: Groups tend to enter the negotiation process with a win or lose mentality

_____ D: There's a lack of motivation on the team's part to want to live peacefully with each other

_____ E: A lack of responsible behavior on the part of the leaders, allowing them to maintain their own 'power positions' rather than addressing the challenges at hand

10. In coping with conflict between others on your team, you would:

_____ A: Anticipate areas of possible resistance and prepare your response before conflict actually develops

_____ B: Urge colleagues to identify possible areas of conflict in advance and seek areas of potential compromise

_____ C: Understand that conflict happens and identify shared concerns and goals

_____ D: Foster harmony on the grounds that the only result of solving the conflict will be the destruction of existing relationships

_____ E: Bring in an impartial arbitrator

SCORING

Add up your scores in front of each letter, "A", "B", "C", "D", and "E". You will end up with a total for each of the 5 letters. To double-check your addition: when you add all of the numbers below, your total should equal 120.

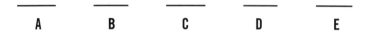

A   B   C   D   E

NEXT:

* ✳ Place a circle around your highest score above
* ✳ Place a box around your second highest score above

⊛ The Five Conflict Resolution Styles

There are five possible styles that we use to problem-solve and deal with issues under stress and in conflict.

Your highest score is how you operate as problem solver. It is your second highest score that illustrates how you deal with conflict or stressful situations. Below is the key to the different styles and what they mean.

(A) DOMINATOR	In conflict, this is a person who believes that he / she is correct, and they will win.
(B) COMPROMISER	In this situation, a compromiser believes that he / she is accomplishing a win; in reality, both parties feel as though they were forced to give something up, and thus both sides will feel less than satisfied.
(C) COLLABORATOR	This is a person who in all circumstances looks for a benefit for all parties, creating value for the other side as well as his/her own.
(D) APPEASER	This person believes that the only solution is to allow the other person or persons to have their way. In the short term, this can be beneficial to quickly solving a problem. In the long term, little is actually accomplished.
(E) WITHDRAWER	When believing that he/she will lose the conflict, he/she will remove him/herself from the situation.

Handling conflict should be done delicately, as a bad or escalated conflict can do permanent or near-permanent damage to a team's cohesion and level of trust with one another.

✸ Using R.E.S.P.E.C.T. to Work Through Conflict

There are three basic scenarios in which conflict occurs:

- ✳ Between yourself and another person
- ✳ Between two others when you are an observer or leader
- ✳ Among the entire team

Regardless of the conflict situation you find yourself in, working through the **R.E.S.P.E.C.T.** model works to eliminate the escalation of the conflict and thus allows a peaceful resolution for everyone.

R: Review the Situation

By reviewing the situation, you may realize that there is no real conflict present. If you do find that you have a conflict arising, then move on to "E."

E: Explore All Possible Solutions

Everybody needs to be involved in exploring solutions. You might even call this a brainstorming session. This stage is about brainstorming possible solutions; it's not about solving the problem.

S: Solving the Problem

This is the phase where you figure out what solutions will work. Everyone involved in the conflict needs to be involved in the solution. When everyone is involved in the solving process, the buy-in is stronger from everyone.

P: Prepare to Follow Through.

Once you have a solution to the problem, you need to follow up to make sure it actually works. This is easily done with benchmarks and specific dates and times to be met.

E: Expect Cooperation

This is a critical step in the **R.E.S.P.E.C.T.** process and should never be taken lightly. This is where everyone opens up about what they expect from each other.

In my workshops, I set up a scenario where I model a conflict situation with a single person. When we get to this phase, I say to the person "This is what I expect from you," and wait for their response. In many cases, the person says OK. This is where significant challenges can arise.

Let's say that Jeff and Caroline are having conflict around a way to approach a solution at the help desk. They have gone through the process of **R.E.S.P.** and are now at the Expect Cooperation stage. Caroline says, "Jeff, this is what I expect from you." Jeff should respond with, "OK, Caroline, and this is what I expect from you." Too often, this does not occur, so when Caroline makes her statement and Jeff only responds with "OK", Caroline then needs to be proactive and say, "Jeff, what do you expect from me?" This allows Jeff, who may be a little more reserved than Caroline, to feel more comfortable speaking up and the process can then continue.

C: Confirm Agreement

Everyone confirms that they agree on the solution and that they will cooperate. This is a confirmation that everyone is on the same page. Sometimes this is best accomplished by having everyone sign an agreement. There is something about signing something that generates greater buy-in.

T: Tracking Mechanism

This is the way we are assured that the resolution was followed through on. It is connected to the "P" which was 'prepare to follow through.' The "T" is the actual process of tracking the progress. Make sure that everyone is communicating throughout the process, and that deadlines are being met and acknowledged. If not, then it is time to regroup.

It is only the Beginning…

Congratulations! You made it to the end of the team half of the book. You now have the tools to help build a cohesive team and be an effective team member. As we discussed early in the book, a ship needs a strong and trustworthy captain to get its ship, crew, and cargo to their destination.

Continue reading the second half of the book. What you will find on the leader half are some of the same sections you found here, just presented from a different perspective — that of a team leader. The two halves of this book are meant to provide you the necessary components of an effective team from both sides of the same coin.

In many of my workshops over the years, one of the most frequent questions that came from frontline employees was, "Are our managers going to get this same training? They need to hear the same message." That is the purpose of this book: getting everyone on the same page and moving in the same direction: One Team, One Dream

T   Success begins with **TRUST**
E   Results "happen" with **ENGAGEMENT**
A   Mutual **ACCOUNTABILITY**
M   Passion for the **MISSION**
S   **SYNCHRONIZE** across lines

R   Focus on **RESULTS**
O   100% **OWNERSHIP** of actions
C   **CULTURE** is core
K   Share your **KNOWLEDGE**

ONE
DREAM
ONE
TEAM

Indispensable Teamwork Skills
to Create a Collaborative Culture

GREGG GREGORY

Contents

Chapter 1 - The Journey Of An Effective Team | **L•1**

Mindset of a Leader | L•2
A Team Culture That Works | L•3
TMVDC | L•5
True North | L•5
Finding Your North Exercise | L•6
Variation | L•8
Magnetic North | L•9
Deviation | L•11
Deviation Experiment | L•12
Compass | L•13

Chapter 2 - Components Of An Effective Team | **L•17**

Four Stages of Team Matriculation | L•17
Leader Types | L•19
Leadership Assessment | L•21
Building a Team | L•25
Be Prepared for Change | L•27
The FUD Factor | L•28

Chapter 3 - The Behaviors Of An Effective Team | **L•31**

MBWA | L•31
Cohesiveness | L•32
Followerrship | L•35
Developing Company Loyalty | L•36
Capability and Readiness | L•38

Skill   L•39

Will   L•40

Capability and Readiness — What Is It?   L•41

Increasing Will   L•45

Intrinsic vs Extrinsic   L•48

Leveraging Feedback   L•50

Performance Standards   L•50

Wheel of Balance™   L•52

Employee Feedback   L•57

When It Isn't Good News   L•60

Chapter 4 - Effectively Leading A Successful Team   **L•63**

Leading with Everything DiSC   L•64

Knowledge Centered Environment   L•67

VDIs   L•67

Effective Meetings   L•69

Avoiding LRS — The Lone Ranger Syndrome   L•75

Managing Conflict Like a Champ   L•78

Final Thoughts   L•86

How to Use *This* Book

If you have not read the team half of this book, do yourself a favor and start over in that section. Even though both halves of the book are stand-alone, it is my intention for the reader to read the team half first, to get that perspective, before diving into the leadership role.

Even if you are not currently in a leadership position, you owe it to yourself to read this half of the book, as you never know what the future holds. It will provide you with a head start for understanding how a leader and team members can work hand-in-hand to strengthen and grow a team. Additionally, it can help you and your team leaders make sure you are on the same page.

The title for the first half is **One Team — One Dream.** On this half, the idea is **One Dream — One Team**. The idea is that the direction of the team begins with a strong and focused leader. The dream of a great team begins at the top.

Chapter 1 The Journey Of An Effective Team

Growing a successful team takes hard work, determination, and, most importantly, a strong strategic approach.

On the team half of the book, we discussed how a leader is like the captain of a ship. They are responsible for their crew and the passage of their ship. In this half of the book, we will discuss how a leader can help foster and direct their crew without necessarily managing their every move. When a leader helps support and foster a winning team, they can guide and consult. They can chart the course and lead the team rather than "run" the day-to-day operations of the crew.

There is a lot of pressure on the captain to make the right decisions. They are so invested in the success of the ship and the journey that if the ship goes down, the captain will save the crew and go down with the ship. As an effective leader, have you ever had to take the heat for something that your team did or perhaps failed to do?

> *"If anything goes bad, I did it. If anything goes semi-good, we did it. If anything goes really good, then you did it. That's all it takes to get people to win football games for you."*
>
> **—BEAR BRYANT**

It is essential that a leader take their role seriously, and understand that they must commit to consistently improving themselves. It is not enough to read one book, or take one class. You have to commit to life-long learning and growing so that your team can grow too. Remember, if you are not growing you are dying.

I was visiting a friend of mine who had a four-year-old son. His son was growing some grass seeds in a cute little pot shaped like a hedgehog. The boy was a little distraught because the pot had broken and was in pieces. His father asked, "Did you drop the pot?"

The boy shook his head and said, "No, dad. It was the grass seeds that did it."

"How did the grass seeds break the pot?"

The little boy smiled and said, "When the seeds grew, the pot was no longer big enough to contain them. When they expanded, the pot broke."

The people on your team are like the seeds. You have to give them room to grow and expand. This means you have to grow and expand with them or the team may be too contained and something will eventually break.

This half of the book was created to help you navigate your team more efficiently and successfully, by walking the pathways I have set forth for you.

✸ Mindset of a Leader

On the team side of the book, we explored the three zones we all have — Comfort, Growth, and Panic zones. Leaders will find themselves in these zones as well. Leaders can easily slip into a comfort zone mentality. Most leaders get their first, and sometimes their second, leadership roles because they did their jobs well, and we know that doing a job well does not necessarily translate into leading others effectively. They can easily fall into a comfort zone and rest on their past success.

Teams need leaders to help pull them into their growth zone and, if the leader is not prepared, everyone can quickly be dragged into a panic zone. You cannot expect followers to live in their growth zone if you, as the leader, are not leading by example.

Though it is much easier to rest on your laurels and stay in the comfort zone, as a leader, you need to constantly make sure that you are stretching your limits and living in your growth zone. You must be trying new things, especially when you get new people on the team.

In order to lead others, you must know how you will operate under pressure. There are always storms and other challenges that a leader will face that can alter the course of the team. Before you set foot in front of your team, you must know what zone you are currently operating in. We constantly fluctuate from zone to zone, even though our goal is to be in the growth zone most of the time. Keep in mind that none of us exists in that state indefinitely. It is important to know where you are before addressing where your team is. Remember, you are leading by example, and you want to avoid leading from hypocrisy.

In addition, it is vital for you to understand what zone your team members typically reside in. This way, when a challenge arises, you will have a clearer understanding of how they may react.

In order to be a successful leader, you can't think like the leaders of yesterday, you have to think differently. You have to break out of that comfort zone because, if you don't, you will get into a routine and that routine will become a rut.

> ## "The only difference between a rut and a grave is about six feet."
> ### – ZIG ZIGLAR

A Team Culture That Works

Merriam Webster defines the word 'culture' as a way of thinking, behaving or working that exists in a place or organization. Many organizations have a long-standing culture, and an individual team's culture must be congruent with the overall culture and values of an organization. These cultures typically flow from the top down.

A strong culture gives each person a purpose, so it is important to align the team culture so that everyone feels valued and included. When the culture and values are established and subsequently utilized, then decisions are much easier.

J. Willard Marriott's original company culture was called the spirit to serve. It is their culture of serving that permeates everything they do internally and externally. It is still their driving force.

Chic-fil-A has a culture surrounding family values. That's why they're closed on Sundays. Malls have wanted Chic-fil-A to have their stores in their food courts, and told them that they had to stay open seven days a week. This was against the Chic-fil-A culture and they refused. If you walk into any mall on Sunday, you will see that the Chic-fil-A restaurants are closed like all of their stand-alone restaurants.

In the last few years, many companies have decided to begin Black Friday retail sales on Thanksgiving afternoon and all night. The retail chain REI decided that, beginning on Black Friday in 2015, they would give their employees the day off to shop. They did not open on Thanksgiving, or the day after. Part of their culture is that they take care of their employees. This did not hurt them at all. According to GeekWire.com, REI's choice to close their retail stores on Black Friday paid off with a 26% rise in online traffic. The added publicity they received was another benefit.

The Hillstone Restaurant Group owns a group of restaurants some of which are called Houston's, along with several others, and has a very strong corporate culture. They're so particular about hiring that they once interviewed about 1100 people to hire only 50. People wanted to be a part of their organization because of the culture of taking care of their employees and their high standards. Because of their high standards, they are one of the most successful restaurant groups in the United States today.

We've discussed a lot about the corporate culture in this chapter, and the fact that even the smallest of teams have a culture. It is this culture that defines either the success or failure of a team. As the leader, what culture are you establishing?

TMVDC

> *"I find the great thing in this world is not so much where*
> *we stand, as in what direction we are moving."*
>
> OLIVER WENDELL HOLMES, SR.

My father taught me how to navigate on an old fishing boat on the Chesapeake Bay in the 1960's, before there was anything known as global positioning satellites. We navigated using a compass and maps to plot our course.

TVMDC is a well-versed formula used for years by both sea captains and pilots to chart and navigate their courses. In order to help you navigate your team smoothly, I have adapted this tried-and-true navigational process to business leadership. So what is TVMDC?

True
Variation
Magnetic
Deviation
Compass

The words are simple; the explanation, powerful. Like any journey, we need a point of reference to begin. As with charting a course on the water, when you are driving your team, you need a point a reference, a place to start. In both navigational principles and business principles, TVMDC begins with True North.

● True North

True North is determined by looking in the sky and finding the star, Polaris. The location of this star is in the handle of the Little Dipper. You can find it by using the pointer stars in the bowl of the

Big Dipper, Dubhe and Merak (bottom of the bowl). Draw a line between these two stars and extend it outward (think out of the top of the bowl) and you will eventually arrive at Polaris. Polaris is the celestial body that marks True North. Polaris does not shift in the sky (from our perspective on Earth); it is always in the same place in the sky. No matter what time of the year, or time of night, you will see Polaris in the same place in the sky. Consider it your anchor to figure out any other direction; to your right is east, to your left is west, and directly behind you is south.

People used this star before there were such things as compasses or maps. This was a fixed spot from which to navigate, compared to Magnetic North, which, as you will learn later, does shift over time.

True North, in business, means Mission, Vision, and Values. These ideals anchor everything else for your team. True North is the point on the map your team is moving toward, and the principles they will follow, with you at the helm. Like the North Star, it is a fixed point.

✸ Finding Your North Exercise

Try this is exercise in a team meeting.

Preparation: You will need a space in which people can move around a bit. Prior to starting the exercise, you will need a standard compass to determine where north is.

1. Ask your team to stand up and spread out (about 5-6 feet apart if possible), then have them close their eyes. Make sure they are not too close to another person, table, chairs, or a wall. Also, make sure no one has vertigo or may lose their balance with their eyes closed. If they do – ask them to be an observer and not actually participate in the activity.

2. Once their eyes are closed, give your team some unique directions. In my workshops I often use some of the following:

* Men turn 90 degrees to the right
* Ladies turn 90 degrees to the left
* If your commute to and from work is less than 30 minutes turn 45 degrees to the left.
* More than 30 minutes turn 90 degrees to the right
* If your favorite topping on a pizza involves any form of meat turn 180 degrees
* *Make up one or two more that would be fun and unique for your team or geographic area.*

3. Keeping their eyes closed, ask your team members to extend their right arm, rotate their entire body and point north.   Inevitably, someone will point straight up in the air. Have fun and say, "Up does not count." Remind them to keep their eyes closed and their arms extended.

4 Take note on how everyone is facing and ask your team to open their eyes. Chances are, many will be facing in different directions.

5. Have your team focus on the fact that they are pointing in many different directions.

6. Explain to the team that this is what can happen if everyone is doing their own thing and they are not focused on a common goal. In this case, they may not have a clear idea where the team currently resides, and even less knowledge of the direction they are heading.

7. Remembering from your preparation step where north is, now you turn and point to north and show the correct direction to your team. Next, have your team all point in the same direction - - -> North.

8. Ask your team, "How does pointing in the same direction look and feel? Do you now feel that you are on the same page, and moving in one direction as one team?"

The question now becomes, how do you, as a leader, chart your own course as well as the course of your team?

✳ Variation

The next letter in TVMDC is V, for Variation. Variation is the magnetic variation on the Earth that changes, and it is a predictive change. Magnetic headings are what we use compasses for, and this shifts over time. The variation is the difference between True North and Magnetic North. Variation is something we cannot control — it is predetermined.

While True North never changes, over time, the Magnetic North "Pole" moves due to the movement of magma under the Earth's crust. Magnetic North moves depending on where you are on Earth. This movement, and how it affects Magnetic North, is something we can observe, just as we can observe a sunset in the evening. While we know the annual variation changes, we simply cannot control it. We can measure it and calibrate accordingly, then make the necessary adjustments.

Have you ever looked at the runway numbers at an airport and wondered what they mean?

At Reagan National Airport (the closest commercial airport to Washington DC), the main runway numbers are 19 and 1. Put a zero at the end of the runway number and it is the approximate compass setting. When you take 19 and place a "0" at the end, you get 190 degrees, which represents an approximate compass heading. If your plane takes off from this runway, you are heading almost due south. The runway number relates to the compass direction that the runway points toward. The other runway number is exactly opposite in direction. In the case of Reagan National Airport — the opposite runway is 10, meaning approximately 10 degrees, or almost north.

According to Kathleen Bergen, spokeswoman for the FAA Southern Region, in *How Changes in Magnetic North Are Impacting Airports*, she states "Adjustments to runways like this and to navigational aids are ongoing. Every five years, the FAA reevaluates shifts in the pole — its magnetic variation — and makes changes to runways and flight procedures as needed." When the variation is more than 3 degrees, the FAA has the airport change its runway numbers.

In the case of Reagan National Airport, a number of years ago, the runway numbers were 18 and 36. However, due to the magnetic variation pulling on the earth, it went beyond the three-degree variation mark. A decision was made by the FAA to change the runway numbers from "one - eight" to "one - nine" and from "three - six" to "one."

In business, there are also variations; things that happen to a company or a team that are beyond your immediate control. One of the most common is when companies merge and the culture of two teams or organizations have to become one.

How can variation affect your team? How has variation affected your team in the past? How can you ensure you are prepared for future variations?

One excellent example of something occurring beyond the control of the average employee is the story of the communications company — Sprint. Before 1984, when government broke up the monopoly on long distance providers, United Telecomm wanted to compete. They had developed fiber optic lines, but they couldn't use them because AT&T owned all of the telephone poles. This monopoly was something that United Telecomm could not control, so they had to adapt their thinking a bit.

They came up with a solution to overcome their variation dilemma. They still had to figure out where to put their fiber optic lines. They collaborated with Southern Pacific Railroad, because they owned the land rights and systems set up for communication on the railroad. As partners, they could use the existing system, and with that partnership in place, they needed a new name. They conducted an internal contest and the winner was Sprint, which stands for Souther Pacific Railroad Internal Networking Telephony.

Sprint had their True North — they wanted to be a competitive long distance telephone company, and recognized they had to chart their course by calculating the variation. They overcame it and, subsequently, they owned it.

✸ Magnetic North

You now have your True North, which is your mission, vision, and values. After factoring in the variation, you can identify the "M" or

Magnetic North for your team. Remember that Magnetic North shifts due to magma shifts under the earth's surface. The concept of Magnetic North is something we can use, day or night, to navigate using our internal compass.

In the earlier exercise, your compass was actually pointing to Magnetic North and not True North. Imagine that you had charted your course on True North, and your compass is pointing to Magnetic North. After even a short distance, you would be off course. Now you can see how critical it is to chart accordingly.

Magnetic North represents the current bearing of your team. This is the direction your team is currently headed. You need to know this in order to keep yourself and your team on course and headed in the right direction. You need to learn how to navigate, calculating for the variation, those things you cannot control. Understanding this will help you navigate towards your True North goals.

The image above is my business logo for Teams Rock. What unique aspect do you notice about this logo? It is tilted 11 degrees to the left. Any idea as to why this very specific angle? Read on.

I mentioned earlier that my father taught me to chart and navigate courses on the Chesapeake Bay, near Annapolis Maryland. The tilt in my company logo is an 11-degree variation to the West, which represents magnetic north near Annapolis.

Suppose you were on a boat on the Chesapeake Bay and you had a compass in your hand. If you faced Polaris (True North), your compass would point 11 degrees to the west, just like my logo.

Remember, unless you are near Annapolis, Maryland, the variation where you are now is different, and the variation from division to division within a company or government agency differs similarly. The image below is a 'compass rose' from a navigational chart of the Chesapeake Bay near Annapolis MD. If you look you can see the outer ring represents Polaris or True North and the inner circle represents Magnetic North.

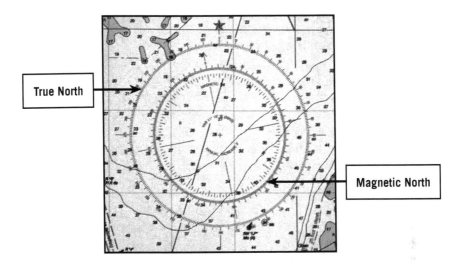

Remember, if you are somewhere else on the planet, and face Polaris, your compass pointer will point to magnetic north from where you are. This is why it is so important to know where you are now, so you can make the necessary course correction and steer your team in the right direction. Understanding your team's magnetic north will let you chart a course and track your own success. Without making this correction, you and your team will certainly not attain your True North destination — your goals.

Keep in mind that unless you are a small company, you are not the only team in a company. You need to know how your team fits with other teams in the company to support the mission. Like gears in a watch, if one team is not working well with others, it is possible that all of the gears will lock up. There has to be integration, communication, and precision between teams.

All of this takes a bit of observation and analysis on your part as the leader. If you are the captain of your ship, you cannot fall asleep at the wheel while the boat is in motion. You have to be mindful and diligent.

☸ Deviation

The next letter in TVMDC is "D" for Deviation. Once you have a clear understanding of the variation your team encounters, next comes deviation. When my dad installed a new radio on his boat, he knew it would affect the compass. Why? Because the radio was mounted near the helm, is made of metal and the speaker has a magnet in it, which created its own magnetic pull. The closer that pull is to your compass, the greater the effect on the compass will be. This action is called compass deviation. Unlike variation, which you have no control over, with deviation, you typically have complete or at least significantly more control. Dad could decide where to put his radio — and he did.

To increase your team's success, you need to understand the strengths and weaknesses of your team members. Knowing what your team is dealing with, both externally and in their interactions with each other, will determine the way you interact together. This is part of knowing where your team is now, mentally and emotionally, and how they will react when variables occur during their journey.

✸ Deviation Experiment

In order to see how deviation can affect your reading of magnetic north, get the compass you used earlier. Next, take your cell phone, computer speaker, or any other device that may have a magnet in it. The bigger the magnet, the greater the visibility of this exercise. Place it near the compass and then slowly move it around.

If you have a smart phone, you can try a variation of this. Open the "Compass" App. Place your phone on a flat surface. Take a magnet (a refrigerator magnet will do) and move it around your phone. Don't use a strong magnet as this could have undesired effects.

What happens?

The magnet moves the compass pointer around. It is a strong magnetic force and, the closer to your compass, the greater the affect. Before dad installed a new radio in our boat, he took a compass reading. After installing the new radio, and without moving the boat, he would take another compass reading and the difference between the two readings would give him the deviation, or how many degrees he had to account for when charting a course.

To make sure we were correct, we would go out on a pre-determined course where we knew the exact magnetic direction (we got this from the current navigational charts) and take a reading on our compass, noting the difference between that reading and the magnetic direction on the navigational chart. That number represents the deviation. We then knew what course adjustments we needed to make.

This is not something that he had to do repeatedly. Once a deviation was determined, it was consistent, unless he added or removed any magnetic devices near the compass; we could clearly see how far off course we were and that would determine what we needed to do in order to get back on course. Our path would be stable at that point. Just to make sure nothing had shifted, he would periodically double-check his adjustments.

In business, deviation is about making adjustments to those things you have control over such as: the projects you work on, the people on the team, how you're going to accomplish the project, the direction of your team, and whether the team agrees on the process necessary to reach the goal. This is the critical part. You have to be sure everyone is pointing, or headed, in the same direction and make the necessary adjustments.

Keep in mind that, in business, your deviation may change simply when a new member joins the team or a new project is assigned. Be ready, be proactive, and be flexible.

Compass

The final letter is "C" for Compass. After you have calculated your variation and deviation, you now have your compass heading. As a leader, it is imperative that adjustments for both variation and deviation are taken into account so the team will be on the correct course and attain the desired results.

On dad's boat, knowing our compass heading would allow us to chart and stay on course to our destination. By tracking our course, we could tell when we were off course. My question to you is, "How can you know when you are off course? How do you know the direction without some instrument guiding you?"

What our ancestors figured out is that there was a great flaw in celestial navigation. You could only really use it at night, unless you were using the sun, but even the sun changes position in the sky depending on where you are and what time of the year it is. Therefore, the compass was a huge leap in technology, even in its simplicity. It points toward magnetic north no matter what time of day, where you are in the world, or the season.

You must have a corrected compass heading to know where your team is headed and what course corrections you may or may not need to make due to potential deviations and variations that appear on the horizon. As things change, a successful leader makes the appropriate course corrections.

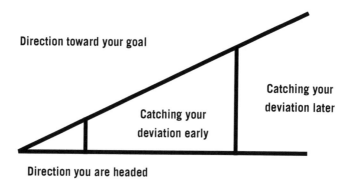

In this graphic, the line heading upward is the direction of your goal, or True North. The line on the bottom is the direction you and your team may be headed without effective deviation course corrections

As you can see, the distance needed to make a correction is relatively small in the beginning (first small vertical line). As time progresses, you are farther away from the direction of your goal and so it will take more time and effort to make a correction. The longer you wait to make corrections, the more difficult those corrections will become.

To ensure you are on the correct course, you need to check your compass from time to time, especially if you are experiencing variables. When a plane is flying from point A to point B on a previously charted course, the pilots may make hundreds, or thousands, of small in-flight corrections because it is much easier (for the flight crew and passengers) to make small, even micro adjustments rather than large ones.

Knowing the direction you and your team are headed, at any point in time, is essential. Once you know where you are, you can chart a course to where you want to go. Remember, you cannot lead until you know where you are going. Taking the time to get your bearings can help you avoid challenges and obstacles as well as identifying which direction your team is growing. Do you recall the boy and the pot of grass seeds? He planted the grass in a larger pot so that it could grow and grow without allowing for the change.

Just as we did in the team side, we are going to break down the parts of a team, but in a modified way. We are going to look at what a leader needs to build a team from the bottom up.

Chapter 2 Components of An Effective Team

On the team side of the book, we discussed my definition of a team. For convenience, I am sharing it again here for you:

A group that trusts and respects each other:

* ✳ Possesses harmonizing skills
* ✳ Is committed to a unified mission
* ✳ Pursues performance objectives or the mission via an agreed upon course
* ✳ Holds each other accountable

I present this as my definition, in hopes that it will help keep you focused on your compass heading. Each part of this definition is in the wheelhouse of what a leader needs to facilitate with. This side of the book will help you do just that, and there must be a commitment to do it. While it is desirable to grow a self-governing team, in order to move the team toward its goal, you must guide them in the early stages. In the team side of the book, I introduced you to the Four Stages of Matriculation. I present them here, again, from your vantage point as the leader.

✸ Four Stages of Team Matriculation

By now, you and your team are in your growth zones and you and your team have identified the team's values and vision. As a leader, it is important to be able to identify what stage your team is in, so that you can apply the right strategies for encouraging growth and working through conflict.

Here are the stages of Matriculation once again. You might want to refer back to the team side for their introduction.

* Forming
* Storming
* Norming
* Performing

In the **Forming** stage, team members ask many questions similar to:

* Who's responsible?
* Why are we doing this?
* What's the purpose of this?

In the **Storming** stage, there starts to be more in-fighting, sub-teams develop, and petty conflict ensues.

In the **Norming** stage, people begin to agree to get along. They agree to set aside differences to move forward.

In the **Performing** stage, people are clicking. While there can be good-natured ribbing, it's not like the Storming phase where there is cat fighting. At this stage, people are working harder, working longer, stress levels are higher, and yet the fun quotient is through the roof.

Which stage is your team in currently?

☐ Forming
☐ Storming
☐ Norming
☐ Performing

What do you think are the next steps to get your team to the next stage?

Do some brainstorming with your team. Get their input about what they think will help them move to the next step. Ask them what you, as a leader, can do to help facilitate their growth. You can also ask other leaders within your organization for their input.

Remember, the goal is to help them self-regulate a bit with you helping them along the way, depending on which stage they are in. In the Forming stage, you may need to be more hands-on but, as you move along the continuum towards Performing; you can relinquish some of that control.

In the next section, you will learn about the different leadership styles and how they are best utilized in the different stages of your team.

✳ Leader Types

A leader, no matter what stage their team is at, must learn the difference between managing and leading.

Traditional thinking states that you manage things and you lead people. Think of it this way; you manage the time sheets, the reports, and projects, but you lead the members on the team.

There are four types of leaders that can be identified. The style you utilize depends on your team's current matriculation stage. The first three levels of leadership are:

* ✳ Authoritative
* ✳ Participative
* ✳ Free Reign

I know there are only three types listed here — stay tuned for the fourth one shortly.

An authoritative leader is a General Patton type (tough and with a lot of grit) while, on the other end of the spectrum, is the free reign leader, or a Gandhi type (quiet and peaceful). The participative leader is in-between. All are very effective, and in order to be effective as a leader, you will need to utilize all three leadership styles appropriately. The style you utilize depends on the matriculation stage of your team.

The authoritative leader typically uses position power. Team members do what they do because they have to, not because they want to. This leader gets things done in a quantitative fashion. They're very efficient, although they are not always effective motivators.

Participative leaders focus more on using their personal power. They start to engage and get people more involved in the decisions. People begin to do things because they want to, not just because they have to do it.

An authoritative leader might say, "John, you need to get this done by Friday." They are very direct, and to the point. The participative leader might say it this way, "John, in the past you have done an excellent job with___, and I would like to have you take point on . . ."

The participative leader engages the employee whereas the authoritative leader issues tasks and directives. There is nothing wrong with either – they are just different.

The free reign leader is a "hands off" leader and allows team members to make decisions. The free reign leader lets team members make the decisions while the leader is primarily a resource. They delegate and let the team run on their own.

Now, there's a myth out there that says that all teams are self-directed. The fact is that teams can become self-directed with the right leadership.

What type of leadership style do you think you primarily use?

☐ Authoritative
☐ Free Reign
☐ Participative

In order to help you gain clarity, here is a simple leadership assessment. It will help you determine where you tend to operate in the spectrum of leadership. Keep in mind, there is no right or wrong answer – just different. After you have your score, we will discuss how to adapt your style.

✳ Leadership Assessment

This assessment indicates your natural or "go-to" style of leadership. An effective leader typically shifts between different styles as necessary during the team's matriculation.

You may also download a PDF file of this assessment online at **http://Bonuses.TeamsRock.com**

Instructions:

Answer each of the questions with Yes, Sometimes, or No.

When you are done, use the scoring index provided. Again, there are no correct or incorrect answers. There is no winning or losing score.

Your score can range from 0-56.

1. Is it worth it for you to take the time to explain your reasons behind a decision before you put into effect?

☐ Yes
☐ Sometimes
☐ No

2. When meeting a new employee for the first time would you ask their name rather than introducing yourself first?

☐ Yes
☐ Sometimes
☐ No

3. Do you believe the most effective means of discipline is to have a strong punishment for violators?

☐ Yes
☐ Sometimes
☐ No

4. Do you keep your team members updated on company and team developments?

☐ Yes
☐ Sometimes
☐ No

5. Is it smart for the team leader to stay out of the way of the rest of the team because you believe that being a friend of the employee reduces the respect they will have for you as a leader?

☐ Yes
☐ Sometimes
☐ No

6. In planning a team outing, some members have said that Tuesday is the best day but you know that Thursday is better for everyone. Would you let the team vote rather than you making the decision for yourself?

☐ Yes
☐ Sometimes
☐ No

7. Do you enjoy taking charge?

☐ Yes
☐ Sometimes
☐ No

8. Do you share and sell your views, as opposed to telling everyone you are the boss and what you say is the way it is?

☐ Yes
☐ Sometimes
☐ No

9. Would your choice be to run your team like a machine rather than having personal contacts and open communication?

☐ Yes
☐ Sometimes
☐ No

10. Do you find that the friendlier you are with your team members, the easier it is to lead them?

☐ Yes
☐ Sometimes
☐ No

11. Do you enjoy supervising your team, as opposed to working hands on with your team?

☐ Yes
☐ Sometimes
☐ No

12. Is it easy to fire someone?

☐ Yes
☐ Sometimes
☐ No

13. In delegation, do you set the goals and leave the method on how to accomplish up to the person?

☐ Yes
☐ Sometimes
☐ No

14. Do you get annoyed if a team member challenges your ideas as
    the leader?

☐ Yes
☐ Sometimes
☐ No

TOTAL_____

SCORING INDEX
Questions numbered 2, 3, 5, 7, 9, 11, 12

* Give yourself 5 points for each **yes** answer

All 14 questions

* Give yourself 3 points for each **sometimes** answer
* A **NO** answer gets zero points

Take your total score and plot your score on the graph to the right.
There is no right or wrong location on the graph. Each management
style has its own positive power points as well as challenges,
depending on your individual situation.

The higher your score, the more you are going to be an authoritative leader and, nearer to the bottom, is the free reign leader. This
is your natural leadership style. What you are striving for is a more
situational leadership style. Therefore, depending on the situation,
you may need to lead a little differently.

In between these other styles are participative leaders. These
leaders are vigilant about the needs of their team and are able to adapt
their leadership style up or down the continuum as the particular
situation warrants.

This is just your natural style and helps you identify how you need
to adapt to different situations to become a more successful leader.

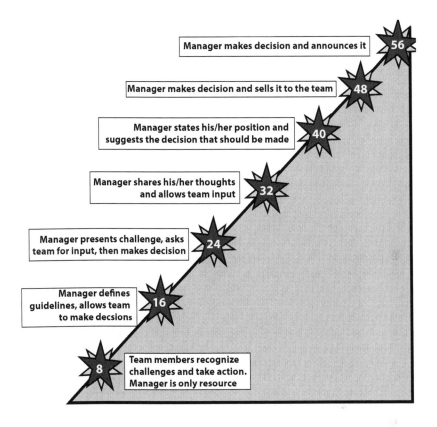

Manager makes decision and announces it — 56

Manager makes decision and sells it to the team — 48

Manager states his/her position and suggests the decision that should be made — 40

Manager shares his/her thoughts and allows team input — 32

Manager presents challenge, asks team for input, then makes decision — 24

Manager defines guidelines, allows team to make decsions — 16

Team members recognize challenges and take action. Manager is only resource — 8

✸ Building a Team

A team in the forming stage really needs to have more direction and thus, a more authoritative leader helps the team form. This is someone who can set the direction, set the tone, and set the rules. In some cases, team members can, and should, help set the team's ground rules and expectations. In some cases, the leader needs to set those ground rules and expectations.

If your team is established, then the team should absolutely help set ground rules cooperatively with you. If it's a project team coming together within an organization, and you are not necessarily involved as a leader in the traditional sense, the team can likely set their own ground rules. On the other hand, if the entire team is newly-hired, then the leader probably needs to set many of the ground rules because he/she may not have knowledge of the people on the team and the team may not have a clear understanding of the organization's mission, vision, and goals. This depends on how well you, as the leader know the members of the team. In many cases, the more input you get from the team members — the stronger and faster the buy-in and the greater the results.

By the time a team reaches the performing stage, the leadership style should be almost completely free reign.

Remember, the free reign leader is a "hands off" leader and allows team members to make decisions. You, the leader, are truly a resource. The free reign leadership style works best when the team is truly a self-directed team in the performing stage. They delegate more and let the team function on their own.

With this in mind, can you imagine what might happen to a performing team if a leader began utilizing more of an authoritative style?

It is what happens between the authoritative and the free reign style that is critical to the successful development of the team. This is where the participative style is most effective. Moving too quickly to free reign or, even worse, starting there, is problematic and a huge challenge to overcome.

If you are not sure where your team is in the matriculation continuum, just listen to keywords the team members are using. If the team members are using the pronoun, "I" or "Me," they tend to be in either the forming or storming stage. If team members are speaking more along the lines of "We," "Us," and "Ourselves," then they are in the norming to performing stage.

When there is a lack of communication, a lack of trust, or confusion, you will probably hear more "I's" and "Me's."

Statements like:

* ✳ "I don't think this is working."
* ✳ "I don't see how this is going to help us."
* ✳ "John is not helping me."

. . . are common in the early stages. On the other hand, statements like:

* ✳ "We're not sure how to make this work."
* ✳ "We are not all adding to the team."
* ✳ "We are not helping each other."

. . . tend to be more team focused.

Even if there is one person causing a problem — the language used is 'We' focused.

 ## Be Prepared for Change

As your team grows and progresses, you need to be prepared for change. These can be very critical times. As the leader, you must be prepared to lead them through change, much as the captain of a ship would help navigate the ship and crew through a storm.

Theorist, Claes Janssen created the concept of the "four rooms of change" to describe what people typically go through when trying to create a change in their life. These same changes occur within your team members.

Comfort

Much like the comfort zone we discussed earlier, this room is where we like to be, unless something causes us to slip into a different room. We are often happy and content here, but no growth occurs. In fact, it is quite possible to stagnate if you stay in this room too long.

Denial

When organizational change occurs, or when something challenges us, we are faced with the idea that, in order to grow, we must change. However, in this room we are in denial. We say things like, "It won't work," or "Management is just testing us. They will never actually follow through." We don't want to move out of our comfort zone and make up reasons to stay there.

Once we accept the inevitable change, we can move forward. If something is not working, we must be willing to try something new. Not only will you grow as a leader, your team will as well.

Confusion

In the confusion room, there is a lot of stress and anxiety. Because you are out of your comfort zone and have accepted that change is inevitable, there is a certain amount of uncertainty and insecurity that can occur. The good news is that this is where creativity happens and you, and your team, become more focused with your energy. When you face your fears of disarray and chaos, new solutions emerge.

Renewal

Finally, when you have found a new way of looking at problems, and new solutions have emerged, you are ready for growth. New possibilities for the future become clearer. You can now relax and gravitate back to your comfort room to celebrate your victory, only to begin the process once again when additional change becomes necessary.

In reality, this process can be quite daunting and intimidating. Once you determine where in the spectrum of change your team is, you can help them move through the process and grow.

The FUD Factor

During the process of change, a team may experience the FUD factor (Fear, Uncertainty and Doubt). As a leader, it is necessary to guide your team through these waters. You do not want FUD to cloud their judgment and influence their decisions and behaviors. Keep things positive, hopeful, and don't forget to celebrate small victories. Change does not occur overnight, and small successes can happen in an instant. When you help your team to recognize these small successes, they will be able to build their confidence, motivation, and momentum.

When change is first announced, morale may actually increase. See the chart on the next page. It is when change begins to actually occur that morale may plummet and the first part of FUD, fear, sets in. Team members are fearful about jobs, functions, and duties.

MOVING YOUR TEAM THROUGH CHANGE

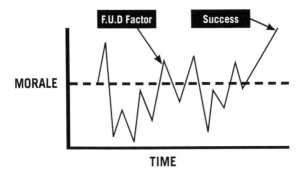

As time progresses, the Uncertainty and Doubt parts of FUD kick in. At this point, team members will show their displeasure regarding the change by expressing uncertainty over whether the change will actually improve anything.

The severity of the change will determine how long it may take a team to move through the FUD process. The greater the change, the longer it takes to move through the process and achieve success. I have seen it take upwards of two years to get a team through this process and other times where the process lasted just a couple of days.

Think about the last new car you bought. When you first drove off the lot, you probably had some challenges with the location of some of the buttons and switches. How long did it take you to get a handle on where things were? Most people get comfortable within a day or two. The FUD process is similar to becoming aware of the newness of your new car.

In the next chapter, we will discuss the behaviors of a winning team. Remember, a team does not exist in a vacuum; they need your guidance and interaction.

Chapter 3 The Behaviors Of A Cohesive Team

Regardless of where you are leading your team, the team will follow, within reason. Team members rely heavily on your assessment and feedback. It is important that you model the behaviors you want your team to follow. In addition, it is important to provide them with feedback (this includes positive and negative feedback) to help them continually adapt their behaviors, increase productivity, and achieve success. In this chapter, we will explore how you, as a leader, can help your team members understand how their behaviors affect the team, the division, and the organization as a whole, and provide them the opportunity to create a more cohesive team.

 MBWA

On the team side, we discussed ABE — Awareness Brings Effectiveness. This is even more critical for leaders. As a leader, you need to pay attention to what is going on with your employees. There is a term you may have heard of that has a couple of different interpretations — MBWA. This is commonly referred to as Management By Walking Around. In some instances, it is sarcastically referred to as Management By Wandering Aimlessly.

MBWA is not meant to be a time to micromanage. This is the time for the leader to observe the team in an unstructured manner, check in with employees and observe progress on active projects. It can even be a time to learn more about an employee on a personal basis or how you might be able to help them grow and develop.

As the leader, you need to be aware of what's going on around you, what the team is doing and what individual team members are doing. It is important to continually learn different things about people on the team. When you open up, let members and colleagues know more about you, allow yourself to be vulnerable, and take time to get to know them, you increase the level of trust with everyone. Some of the items you can get to know about your team include their spouse's name, their dog's name, the names of their children, where they like to go on vacation, etc. In short, the more you know about them and they know about you, the more their level of trust increases. There is a balance here; you should not make your team members feel like Big Brother is watching them. They should feel like, and you should, authentically care about them and their lives. If you are faking it, they will know and trust will be undermined and, possibly, destroyed.

MBWA means maintaining awareness of what people are doing — who is pulling their load and who isn't. Don't wander aimlessly, be sure to move around and interact with purpose. Let your team know you are there for whatever they may need. Be sure to be available to help your team when they need help.

✸ Cohesiveness

According to the Merriam Webster dictionary, the word "cohesive" is defined as *closely united*. As a leader, you have a responsibility to build a cohesive team. A cohesive team is one that fosters a community spirit and team members having a unified vision.

Community spirit is about getting people engaged and involved with the team. It means that everyone can count on everyone else to "have their back." One way this can be accomplished is with activities outside of day-to-day work. Some people will relish this opportunity, while other people will think it's downright stupid. It's finding that mix that effective leaders do very well. Some organizations will take people out and have a bowling night. Others will have a company picnic or a team development day. One company I know of has a spirit day twice a year. They close their offices down for their entire organization and celebrate. While they sometimes bring in a speaker for a couple of hours, the biggest part of the day is about having fun with the whole team. It's about building community spirit. That's the critical part.

Kensington, Maryland is a town many have never heard of, although over the years, they have made national news a few times. Kensington had the spotlight on them because of the DC sniper in October of 2002. In late July of 2002, there was a terrible train wreck that occurred when an Amtrak train headed from Chicago to Washington DC derailed.

Even though the community is readily visible in times of chaos and tragedy, I think about how, through community spirit, the residents of Kensington came together in December of 2001.

Every year, the Kensington Fire Department gives back to the community by putting Santa Claus on a fire truck and riding up and down the streets of Kensington while Santa Claus waves to everybody. Each night, it became a mini-parade in parts of Kensington. Santa also arrived on a fire truck to light the town's Christmas tree. It was a tradition that brought the community together.

In November 2001, the Kensington town council disinvited Santa in favor of Uncle Sam and patriotism. After the attacks on September 11th, everyone was looking forward to the annual tree lighting event, and a sense of normalcy.

Have you ever worked in an organization where there's a mass majority who want to do one thing and a microscopic, yet vocal few who want to do something else? That was the problem facing the town of Kensington. Even with incredible support for Santa Claus, the town council voted not to have him light the town tree.

The locals were outraged and decided to go to the local news media, who would make it a big deal. While it started out as a local story, it was quickly picked up by national, as well as international, media outlets.

Within two days of the story breaking, I received an email from a friend in the US Air Force who was stationed in Germany asking if there was anything that I wanted to share with him about Kensington.

How fast does news travel today? If you said fast, you are right.

Now, how fast does bad news travel? Even faster. For a strange reason that is unexplainable as a society, we love to hear about negativity.

The news outlets touted — Santa Claus is not welcome in Kensington, Maryland. The town council was thrust into the national and international spotlight. They had to do something, and this is what they decided.

"Santa Claus will not light the tree, but he can be present on the stage when the tree is lit."

The night they lit the tree — in addition to more people than had ever attended the tree lighting ceremony, and the incredible number of news media present, countless people came dressed as Santa Claus to show support for their town. Now that is community spirit.

This is the type of community spirit a leader needs to foster on their team to bring everyone closer.

Think about your immediate team. If somebody is out sick, does the rest of the team automatically pick up the slack, or do they wait for management to tell them? Or do they say things like, "Bob's out sick. I'm not doing his work"?

In my workshops, I typically ask if anybody lives on a dead end street, or cul-de-sac? I then ask, "Of the neighbors around you, how many of them do you know on a first name basis including children?"

Inevitably, people will say, "Not that many." Perhaps they will know one or two immediately next door.

I follow this up with, "Do you know what kind of cars they drive."

More often than not, the response is a very strong, "YES, every car."

I then ask the all-important question, "What happens if a strange car drives down the street or into their cul-de-sac?"

They notice it, and typically watch to see where it goes or at what house it stops.

It is not about being nosy. Well maybe a little. In reality, it is more about watching out for your community. On your team, are you all watching out for each other?

In order to truly lead a team, and help them become cohesive, you must have the right team members. They have to trust you and you need to trust them. Team members must trust your ability to lead the team, in the right direction, trust in your vision for the team, and believe that you have the highest level of integrity. You need to trust that your team members will follow your lead, be responsible enough to do their part, and be loyal to their fellow team members. In the next section, we will explore the concept of Followership. You have to pick the right people when hiring new members to your team, and, for those that were there when you became the leader, you must guide and support them to help them become part of a cohesive team. The team cannot do it on their own.

✳ Followership

On the team side of the book, you learned about followership styles - Alienated, Conformist, Pragmatist, Passive, and Exemplary followers credited to R.E. Kelly. Your job as the team leader is to recognize and pay attention to the types of followers you have, encourage the exemplary ones, and work to nurture and develop the ones who may unintentionally hurt the team.

As the leader you must be cognizant of the behaviors exhibited by each of the following types of followers.

Alienated Followers

You'll recognize this person. He or she is the team critic, anxious for attention derived from pointing out all the problems and negative points. This can sometimes be perceived as an attempt to hijack leadership with "better ideas." This person's self-image as that of Robin Hood can prove to be perceived by others as hostile, uncooperative, and perhaps even a threat to team leadership.

Conformist Followers

These members are often referred to as "yes men," following the leader's directives to the letter. They can become problematic when crossed and even zealous in their enforcement of those directives. They often reflect the leader's personal directives, and may have difficulty with others on the team.

Pragmatist Followers

These are the folks who tend to keep their heads down in order to be perceived as players who can be trusted not to rock the boat. The challenge here is that this type of behavior often produces mediocre results. They learn how to apply the rules to their own goals and sometimes take their eyes off the team's objective. On the surface, they may seem like strong team players when, in fact, they tend to be focused on themselves.

Passive Followers

These folks bring little pro-activity to the organization, requiring total supervision. They tend to be clock-watchers, passing through life with the minimum of involvement or contribution. They may be anchors, slowing down progress and taking up valuable seats where more value is needed.

Exemplary Followers

These are your greatest ally, keeping the objective of the group uppermost in their mind and actions, presenting both leadership and team members with a fully honest representation. They tend to have a stronger amount of influence over other members.

✺ Developing Company Loyalty

Having a team of only exemplary followers is not likely to happen. Virtually every team will have a mix of each of these types of followers. Great leaders know how to work with and develop each type of follower to produce the greatest results. It is really up to the leader to inspire team members to want to be part of the team culture, to work for the benefit of their fellow team members and those they serve.

In 1927, when J. Willard Marriott opened his first A&W Root Beer stand in Washington DC, he was dedicated to customer service with his spirit to serve. It was not until about thirty years later that

Marriott opened their first hotel. Marriott was also committed to his employees because he knew that, in order for them to embrace the spirit to serve, they needed to feel like they were an important part of the company. He not only developed a "brand" for the company, but he also created a "brand" for employees. The Marriott franchise continues to be committed to providing competitive wages for employees. J.W. knew that this was not enough to create loyal employees, he had to create a culture in which employees felt like they mattered and that they were part of family.

In 1957, when there was just one hotel, J.W. would often sit in the lobby and talk to the employees. He would sit down on the couch and let them talk about what was personally impacting their lives and he would provide support and advice. As the company grew, he could not be at all places at once, so now, each leader in each department spends 15 minutes each day with their team, to talk through different issues that may be impacting them. They make sure that they celebrate birthdays, anniversaries, and other special events. They are committed to their employees, which, in turn, creates a fierce loyalty.

J.W. did not believe the spirit to serve was something that could be taught from a manual, and in fact, he wanted to hire people based on their attitude toward their guests, rather than their experience in the hospitality industry. He believed hospitality skills could be taught. We will talk more about the development of skills in the next section.

One other thing that developed loyalty and a positive "employee branding" for the company was that the employees are dedicated to hiring from within. They want people for life, and foster their leadership skills in order to help employees feel that they are part of an organization they can grow in. In fact, 50% of the managers at Marriott were promoted from within.

Part of assessing your team's ability to follow you effectively is to determine if they have the skills needed to do their job and, if they don't, do they have the motivation to learn and grow.

A successful leader knows what they need in order to develop a cohesive team; especially when it comes to the skills necessary to produce desired results. In theory, it would begin when you hire and continue during the onboarding process.

❋ Capability and Readiness

In reality, leaders often inherit a team and its members, meaning it is necessary for leaders to know and understand the style of each of their team members, and how they fit within the team.

Leaders must assess whether their team members have the skills (Capability) necessary to perform their job and, more importantly, are they motivated (Readiness) to work to fill in the gaps in their skill set. It is the leader's duty to ensure a team member is up to speed with their responsibilities as this solidifies the team member's position on the team and strengthens the team's cohesiveness from within.

A team member must have the necessary skills to perform the job they were hired to do. They may have been hired with some skills such as certifications, licensure, or other eduction and work experience. Some other skills must be learned and acquired while on the job. It is important for the leader to have a conversation about the expectations for developing these additional skills. The conversation should include expectations of both the team member and the leader to accomplish these training goals.

It is not enough to just identify the skills a team member must develop; they must have the willingness to develop them. The CR assessment can help to identify certain areas to work on, however the team member must have incentive and a drive to be successful in their job. The leader must be aware of what drives their team members and realize that motivation is different for everyone. Some people respond to a pat on the back while others respond to more demonstrative actions such as an announcement to the whole team. (Refer to the section on "Leading with Everything DiSC" on page L•64)

Skill

In order to assess a team member's skill set, consider the following.

* Is the team member experienced at the task?
* Have they received proper education or training on the task?
* Does the team member have a clear understanding of the task?
* Do they have a clear understanding of their role on the team?

Successful Experience at the Task

Successful experience is whether they have had success at the task or a similar task in the past. Just because they worked in a similar position is not indicative of success. It is imperative that you, as the leader, know that they have experienced success at this type of task in the past.

Proper Education at the Task

Proper education at the task means that they have been formally and properly trained. They may have been working on an oil pipeline for years, yet not have a college degree. Their education at the task could be experiential, or even informal, training. Some positions do not require formal education and training. Think about a forklift operator, do they need a master's degree? No, they do need proper education at the task of operating a forklift. Believe me, they are tricky to drive.

Clear Understanding of the Task

Clear understanding of the task is an area that you, as the leader, have to pay attention to. Be sure to ask the team member about their understanding of the task and observe how they perform it.

Clear Understanding of their Role on the Team

Sometimes, a team member is like a cog in a machine. They need to understand their role on the team and how it, along with their assigned tasks, relates to others within the team and the organization as a whole.

✺ Will

Is the team member willing to work to make changes?
Do they have. . .?

* Confidence
* Security of non-threat
* Incentive
* Willingness

Confidence in What They Are Doing

A leader must observe, assess, and regroup with a team member with their observations of how confident the team member is at performing their job. A leader should also ask the team member how they are doing and feeling about their position. If the team member is not confident, the leader should come up with a plan for the team member. It could mean closer shadowing, or more education on the task. Keep in mind that there is a fine line between confidence and arrogance.

Security of Non-Threat

If a team member is always worried about losing their job for messing up, they do not have the "security of non-threat." Being worried and stressed all the time will have a definite negative effect on skill and performance. Their confidence will be undermined and they may begin to make mistakes, and worse not care about it. The team member should be reassured that they are not going to be fired for making a mistake — unless, of course, it's brain surgery!

Clear Incentive

While an incentive of money is nice — clear incentive can be as simple as accomplishing a goal for their performance evaluation, tuition reimbursement, or the satisfaction of knowing that they have done something right for someone else. Key thing to recognize — there are many incentives.

Willingness to See the Job or Task Through to Completion

There has to be a willingness to see the job through to completion. They must want to do a great job and be open to ways to improve and grow. If the employee is only doing the bare minimum to get by, the leader should be creative about how they inspire and motivate the employee to want to work harder.

✸ Capability and Readiness — What Is It?

Capability and Readiness are defined by the team member having the will and the skill necessary to perform specific tasks successfully and within required standards. It is important for you, as a leader, to understand that a team member's ability and motivations are interdependent. This means that the more a team member wants to do something, the better their performance will be.

Using the skill sets above, you can assess the Capability Readiness Factor (CR) for any task.

Capabilities Readiness Factor 4 — CR 4 (High Skill, High Will)

In order for a team member to be considered a CR 4, they must display very strong traits in all four will and skill areas.

Your mission, as the team leader, is to get as many of your team members to the CR 4 level on as many tasks as possible. While you will probably have a small percentage of high skill, high will team members at any one time, it is a goal worth pursuing.

Capabilities Readiness Factor 3 — CR 3 (High Skill, Low Will)

A CR 3 can be viewed as having strong skill traits. They will be lower on the will side of the equation. This is likely your most difficult member on the team. Simply put, they may have the skills necessary to effectively do their jobs, and they just are not motivated to do it. Now be careful. There are varying degrees of will, so do not be too quick to judge. It can be difficult to get somebody with the skill to reignite their will. In short — they may simply be burned out.

Being a CR 3 does necessarily mean they are negative. Assuming they are a good worker, you may need to see if there is another task or position on the team or perhaps a different team altogether, for them. As an organization, you do not want to lose a dedicated employee to burn out.

Several years ago, I had a friend who had gone through a pretty rough divorce and was living outside of the Baltimore, MD area. In the summer, she loved to head to the ocean beaches on the weekend. Several months after the divorce, she said to me that she felt she needed a new job. I said, "But you like your job, and you like the people."

She said, "Yeah, I know, but I've been here for a while and just feel like I need a change, and this one is the most obvious." She was just really in a funk and burned out on a variety of levels. She liked her job, had a high degree of skill and, because she was burned out, her desire, or will, to perform was quite low.

Remember, she liked to go to the beach, and even though it took upwards of five hours to get there, during the late spring and summer months, she'd hop in her car and drive to the beach every Friday. Then fight the traffic back on Sunday night, or sometimes early on Monday morning, and go straight to work. She was being burned out in every sense of the word.

I suggested to her that she go talk to her boss and make an offer to them. Now, keep in mind, she worked with a company that had the flexibility to work with her, and they liked her as well. After I made the suggestion, she said they would never go for it. I just suggested she try, and that she had nothing to lose.

The next day, she called me back and said with amazement, "Oh my gosh, they agreed." What she proposed to them was instead of working Monday through Friday eight hours a day, 40 hours a week, she would now work Monday, Tuesday, Wednesday, Thursday, ten hours a day and she has off Friday, Saturday, Sunday and Monday. She has a four-day weekend and of course heads to the beach.

The next week she would work Tuesday, Wednesday, Thursday and Friday for 10 hours each day, followed by a two-day normal weekend. The following week she works Monday through Thursday and has a four day weekend.

Because she was invigorated by her four day weekends, on her two-day weekends she would often go into the office to knock out some extra work. Her company liked the idea so much that they found a co-worker who liked the concept and they alternated their long weekends. That simple act took at least one, and likely two, employees from a CR 3 and instantly elevated them to a CR 4.

After more than a decade working in the mortgage banking industry, I was a very strong CR 3. I had stepped out of an official leadership capacity and, while I had a very high level of skill, I had simply lost my desire, or my will, to want to do the job. I no longer enjoyed doing the job, and eventually left the industry and began my own speaking and consulting business on teamwork. During this time, I was never negative; in fact, I actually helped train the new hires — I was simply burned out.

Capabilities Readiness Factor 2 — CR 2 (Low Skill, High Will)

A CR 2 is somebody who displays strongly on the will traits but is not observed as having strong skill traits. Most commonly, this is a new hire

Do you remember your first day on a new job? You probably had an incredible level of will and wanted to jump right into the job. While you were excited, and perhaps had some of the skills necessary, this company probably did some things differently than you were used to, thus your level of skill may have been somewhat lower — at least for the time.

If the new hire is brand new to the work force, this may be amplified even more. An example I often use in my workshops is that of a person who comes in and says, "Come on boss, let me at it. I can do it. I know I can do it. It's just a little nuclear reactor. I can handle that." As an effective leader, you need to be careful not to mistake someone's level of will for a skill. This will get you and the team in hot water.

This is why it is critical that, when hiring someone new, that you find that least common denominator of the skill set necessary to do the job, and then place a very strong emphasis on the person's level of will. Remember, in general, it is easier to teach a brand new skill set than increase the level of will in an employee.

When a person has the will to succeed, they will want to learn the skills necessary for them to succeed. In my workshops, I often spend time focusing on the "why" to do something before we focus on the "how." I do this because helping everyone learn the "why" increases their level of will and they are then more ready to understand the skill or the "how." If we begin with the how without understanding the why, the average person will mentally check out. The same applies to your team members. We all have a why behind everything we do.

Capabilities Readiness Factor 1 — CR 1 (Low Skill, Low Will)

The last Capability Readiness factor is a CR 1. This is a person who has both low skill and a low level of will. Let's be completely clear, as a leader, you would never, ever hire somebody that has low skill and low will. Statistically, somewhere down the line in your leadership career, you will inherit somebody like this. So my question to you is, what trait can you raise up to the highest level first? A person's skill or a person's will? Remember, we just talked about hiring the least common denominator and train the skill.

When you have somebody with low skill and low will, the first thing you have to do is to help them achieve some success at a few simple skill sets. Do not give them too much and overwhelm them. Let them master these few, even at the simplest level. Then praise them more than you might think is normal. Let them feel like what they just accomplished makes them the king of the world. By doing this, you will have jump-started their motivation and desire to grow, and you have increased their will. After a couple of times working like this, their will level should grow enough so that their desire to improve increases (aka their will) and in turn, their skill set increases

In short, you increase the level of skill at first, and then the will of the person takes over and drives the skill. If there is no will, they will never grow their skills. So, to answer my question above, you can raise the person's level of will to the highest level first. While you cannot teach this, by encouraging, you are increasing their natural ability to want to do better.

If you cannot get them to grow, they just don't have the will or skill, and are not willing to try, then it may be time to offer some career redirection advice.

Top-tier companies typically spend a lot of time and resources building up their image to hire and retain people through motivators such as competitive wages and by creating a work place that team members look forward to coming to every day. Next, we will explore other ways to motivate both the individual and the team.

✸ Increasing Will

Motivation is something that comes from within and, while this is absolutely true, as the leader, you are tasked with keeping your team moving and motivated. There are things that can motivate both individuals and your team as a whole.

Motivating employees can be a challenge. There are two realities:

1. You cannot motivate anyone who does not want to be motivated.
2. Everyone wants to be motivated.

While this sounds contradictory, I assure you it is not. Simply put, motivation is a change in behavior. The root word motivate is defined by the Merriam Webster dictionary as *"To give someone a reason for doing something."*

Giving someone a reason is not the act of motivating the person. People will change their behavior based on two factors. First is a need, and the second is an emotion. When either of these is triggered in a person, a change in their behavior occurs.

Several years ago, I was traveling through San Francisco International Airport, taking the red-eye flight to Washington DC.

As I walked through the screening area, a TSA agent said, "Hi, how are you?"

It was said in a way that had no energy and sounded as if she was just going through the motions; as if she didn't really care how I was actually doing. Of course, I responded very enthusiastically, "I am doing AMAZINGLY WELL, and getting better."

Her response was priceless, "Well somebody's in a gooooooooood mood," and again, her sarcastic tone of voice betrayed the words she was speaking. My response, "Why would you choose to be in a bad mood?"

Almost immediately, a genuine smile came across her face and she said, "You're right, and thank you for reminding me that it's a choice."

I walked about fifteen feet away, stood behind a large column, and observed her behavior for the next few minutes. Several people in line were greeted with, "Welcome to San Francisco International, how are you this evening?" This time it was said with excitement and enthusiasm.

Did I motivate her? No. What I did was to give her a reason to modify her behavior and, subsequently, motivate herself. The biggest challenge is maintaining this new behavior. In this case, I am quite confident that my actions had a temporary effect. In fact, her mood probably dropped again as soon as she was greeted with a very negative passenger. Vast majorities of us are fickle and allow ourselves to be influenced by others.

Motivation comes from different sources. Sometimes, like in the case of the TSA agent, it was internal. I only reflected her mood; I did not motivate her to change her demeanor — that she did on her own. Sometimes, motivation comes from external forces, like getting a bonus at the end of the week for exceeding sales.

Intrinsic vs Extrinsic

There are two real types of motivators — intrinsic and extrinsic. Both are very valuable and useful at the appropriate time. The key is knowing when and how to use each type and with whom they will have the greatest impact.

Extrinsic motivators are things that exist outside of you and that you might want such as money, food, position, title, etc. Extrinsic motivators absolutely work. The challenge with the extrinsic motivator is that the effect of motivation lasts only as long as the extrinsic value is present, and recognized. Once the value is gone, so too is the new behavior.

Intrinsic motivators are the things that stimulate you from within such as knowledge, responsibility, recognition, and accomplishment. For instance, if a company offers tuition reimbursement for college courses, this would be an intrinsic motivator for those employees who are pursuing higher education. While there is an extrinsic component, it is an intrinsic value because it's something that will help them increase their knowledge. Think of it this way, if there is an emotional component to the action, it is intrinsic.

According to Abraham Maslow in his 1943 paper, "A Theory of Human Motivation" there is a sort of pyramid of needs. We cannot meet a particular set of needs until we have met the needs of the level below. For instance, if you do not have a house and food, you will not do very well trying to maintain social or romantic relationships. We are motivated to achieve those needs. This is why the pursuit of money is so strong. We need to meet our most basic needs. These needs are both internal and external, but are driving forces for both leaders and team members.

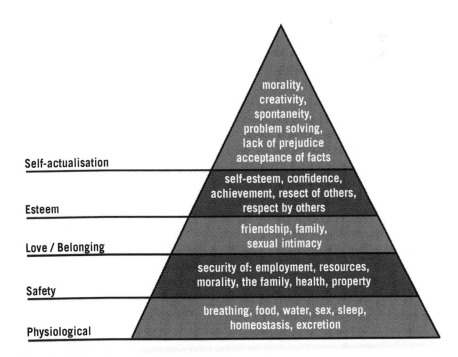

Which has more value to the employee? A leader can give a team member an extra ten dollar bonus or take the time to handwrite a personal note. In short, it depends, if the extra ten dollars is the only way the employee can get home, then the ten dollars has greater value.

An extrinsic motivator is temporary. You spend the money or gift card your boss gave you, and it is gone. Have you ever noticed the thank you cards on the desk of co-workers? People have been known to keep those little cards on their desks for a year or more. All motivators wear off — extrinsic motivators typically wear off more quickly.

As I began to transition from mortgage banking into my speaking career, I had been working with a national mortgage banking company whose regional office was in the greater Atlanta area. I knew I was going to be in Atlanta to meet with one of my speaking clients, so I called a few weeks in advance and we set up a dinner with team members that I had previously only talked with over the phone and never met. One of the transactions I had with this company was with Karen about 18 months earlier. It was the first transaction where we worked together and it was not a simple transaction. After the loan went to closing, I sent Karen a note of thanks, and that I appreciated working with her. Leap forward 18 months, when I went to Atlanta and visited their office before dinner. One of the first things I noticed as I walked by Karen's cubicle was the card I sent her. She saw me looking at the card and told me how much she appreciated the card and that whenever she is bogged down and frustrated, she looks at the card and smiles and that little card motivates her to keep moving forward. That is classic intrinsic motivation.

Below is a list of inexpensive ways to motivate your team.

- ✳ Life Savers candy when someone is a life saver at work
- ✳ Can of Mountain Dew for a "Can Do" attitude
- ✳ A pack of "Extra" (brand name) gum for going the extra mile.
- ✳ Post-it-note of thanks
- ✳ Certificate of appreciation
- ✳ Corporate letter of appreciation
- ✳ E-card — Hallmark.com
- ✳ Paper card — Successories.com

✳ Recognition in front of team — for the right personality type
✳ Private recognition — for the right personality type
✳ Gift certificate to local restaurant – or anywhere else
✳ Physically wash their car
✳ Flowers hand-picked or florist
✳ Take them to lunch — at their favorite place
✳ Create an awards program — the more personalized, the better
✳ Employee of the month parking spot

My Favorites Book

One of my all-time favorite inexpensive motivators is the "My Favorites Book."

Create a simple form with a blank line for the employee to write his or her name, and then ask the employee to answer the questions below. Have each employee complete the document. Feel free to add some of your own — keeping in mind that the cost needs to be very low.

✳ My favorite chocolate
✳ My favorite candy that is not chocolate
✳ My favorite ice cream
✳ My favorite soft drink
✳ My favorite drink that is not a soft drink and non-alcoholic
✳ My favorite topping on a pizza
✳ My favorite flower (specify color)
✳ My favorite fast food restaurant
✳ My favorite casual dining restaurant

If an employee politely says they do not feel comfortable sharing this information, then that is OK. On the other hand, if an employee sounds off and says something like, "My personal information ain't none of your business," then you have a much deeper problem.

Once everyone on the team has completed their sheets, place them in sheet protectors and put them in a three-ring binder. Make sure the binder is easily accessible by everyone, and let them know that any time someone on the team does something special for them, they may go to the My Favorites Book (MFB) and see what you can do for them to show your appreciation and thanks. The key here is to list things of little monetary value that will provide them something they will actually appreciate.

✹ Leveraging Feedback

In the last part of this chapter, we will discuss providing feedback to your employees on a regular basis. To do this right is really essential for two main reasons. First, you want the employee to be clear on the areas they are doing well and areas they need to improve. The other reason is that you want to maintain your employees' strong follow-ership. You want them to continue to trust and respect you.

In motivating employees, they say that one can use a carrot, or one can use a stick. The best leaders use the carrot as much as possible and use the stick sparingly. A way to make sure your team is going in the right direction, and following the carrot, is to have clear expectations. There cannot be guesswork because, inevitably, there will be a misunderstanding or miscommunication. On the team side of the book, you learned about the styles of communication. On this side, we will explore the content and purpose of your communications as a leader. The clearer you are about your expectations with team members, from day one, the better.

It begins with describing what the performance standards are - that is the expectations of the team member's job and how they fit into the team. There is a daily dialogue with team members to reinforce these standards, and if you're like most organizations, there are evaluations that are done with team members, usually yearly, to let them know how they are doing, to reward them for their efforts (carrot), or create a plan of correction if they are not meeting standards (the stick), and make a plan for further growth over the next year.

✹ Performance Standards

Performance standards are not the job description. A job description conveys the reason a job exists. It will outline what is to be done and why. Without strong performance standards, you cannot begin to provide feedback to the employee — either positive or negative.

Performance standards are "rules" you expect an employee to work within as well as the level of performance expected of them. Leaders who utilize the following steps will generally gain a greater commitment from their employees, resulting in a more effective team performance.

Imagine that you are out on a baseball field and you have a target — the catcher's mitt. Think how well you can throw the ball from about 60 feet away (the distance from the pitcher's mound in major league baseball)

If you've got a target in front of you that's 10 feet square (a lot bigger than a catcher's mitt), do you think you could hit it from 60 feet away? Many people I know would say yes. If not, what about if you were just 20 feet or 240 inches away?

Now, what if you were blindfolded and told to make three complete turns, could you hit it? Probably not, or at least your probability drops drastically. When you don't have performance standards in place, it's like blindfolding your employees. They can't hit what they can't see.

Here is a list of some guidelines for effective performance standards:

* Specific criteria such as quantity, and quality of performance and goal achievement. The more quantifiable the standards are, the easier they will be to measure

* Performance standards should be agreed upon between employee and management on a regular basis. By having these standards agreed on by everyone, the greater the buy-in by everyone

* Set all standards to clearly outline how the employee will be measured. It is essential that all measurements be made to the standard and not to others in like positions

* Standards will give the employee a "baseline" for effective performance on the job and outline goals for the future. Once a base line is established, measurement becomes significantly easier

What standards are currently in place for your team? What are a few new standards you would like to put into place? What standards would the team like to implement? Remember that you cannot expect your team members to know exactly what you are thinking and when. Believe me when I say, osmosis does not work in leadership. Understanding performance standards is critical at every level.

✹ Wheel of Balance™

To help with the process of staying in touch, I use the Wheel of Balance. The concept of the Wheel of Balance was something used by one of my early managers in the mortgage banking industry. Over the years, it has evolved into this magnificent tool to help in a variety of areas.

A reality of leadership is that performance reviews are one of the most valuable tools a leader can utilize to help develop an employee and subsequently increase their productivity. Let's face it though, most leaders (and employees) cannot stand doing them or, for that matter, receiving them. The challenge is that most organizations only use performance reviews once a year. What happens during the remainder of the year? Is it put aside and not thought about by anyone? Sadly, in many cases, that answer is yes.

The Wheel of Balance can be used throughout the year as a way to create, assess, measure, and monitor the progress of employee goals throughout the year. It is a collaborative and cooperative process that requires input from both the leader and the team member.

When you use the Wheel of Balance, the usual measuring and monitoring takes significantly less time, helps keep the team member on task, and provides a way for you, as the leader, to keep in touch with each employee's progress. It is easier to tweak a goal every quarter than it is to assess only once a year.

Effectively utilizing the Wheel of Balance allows you to take the goals and objectives from the most recent performance evaluation and cultivate a personal action plan for each employee. By personalizing this plan, you are building a greater level of trust and letting them know the value each individual brings to the team.

3 Steps to Getting the Wheel Rolling

The first use of the Wheel of Balance takes three brief meetings over three days to complete, and there is some homework for both the team member and the leader. Before the initial meeting let the team member know about this process and the time line.

Day 1 (Block out about 20 minutes for a meeting with the employee)

1. Ask the employee to determine the eight key traits he/she feels are the key components to accomplishing their goals for the next year. The employee does this on their own time and should not take more than 30 minutes to complete. Before they leave, make sure that they understand that they will be meeting with you the next day. Be specific about how much time it is expected to take.

2. As their manager or leader, it is important for you to know what key traits are necessary for the employee to be successful at their job so, while the employee is completing their list of key traits for accomplishing their goals for the next year, you will create a similar list of what you believe the employee should have in their top eight key traits.

Day 2 (Block out a meeting with the employee for 60 – 90 minutes)

1. In this meeting, you and the employee will compare your lists. Keep in mind that you will NEVER agree on all eight traits. If you agree on half of them, that is awesome. The strategic value here is to engage with the employee in a real and open dialogue. This helps lay out the overall employee development plan. Here is where you and the employee reach a mutually agreed upon list of eight strategic performance points. Take the time needed to be sure you are both on the same page. This micro-step is essential. It is important that the employee have significant input in the process. This gains buy-in and, ultimately, ownership of the overall process.

2.   Next, you will ask the employees to rate themselves, on a scale of 1 – 10, reflecting how well they feel they are accomplishing each of the eight points that you just agreed upon. (See the index of rating scale below). This should take the employee between 10 and 15 minutes and will be done outside of the meeting in preparation for the next day's meeting.

3.   Once again, you will do the same for the employee. As their leader, you should have a strong idea of their strengths and weaknesses. If you are a new leader to this team, you may need to involve another leader.

4.   Be sure that the employee knows what to expect on Day 3 and what the time commitment will be.

HERE IS THE RATING TABLE GUIDELINES

1. You have never heard of doing this.	6. You know you should do it and do sometimes.
2. You have heard of it but never do it.	7. You see the value and will attempt to do it more.
3. You have heard of it but don't want to do it.	8. You do this on a regular basis.
4. You do it when forced to do it.	9. You do this a majority of the time.
5. You see the benefit but are still reluctant.	10. You live this, both personally and professionally.

Day 3 (Block out a meeting with the employee for 90 minutes)

1.   First, compare your scores with the employee's scores. Like the day before, it is not likely that you will completely agree with each other's scores. It is also not probable that the employee will score themselves as a nine while you give them a score of one. It is likely that there will be a difference of one or two points for most of the eight performance points. This creates a great opportunity to engage in an open dialogue and make sure you are both on the same page as far as expectations. It is important for you to reach a mutual agreement for the scores of all eight items. It is important to note that you do not simply average the scores, and that you and the employee come to a mutually agreed upon score. This is the opportunity for both you and the

employee to voice your opinions and to see clarity in the performance standards we discussed above.

Once you have agreed on the scores, it is time to plot the eight scores to create a visual tool for both the employee and you to refer to. See the wheel on the next page or draw one of your own. You will now plot each of the (mutually agreed upon) eight performance points on a spoke of the wheel. Each spoke can be separated into 10 divisions (from middle to the outer circle. 1 is near the center and 10 is on the outer circle). Move around the circle clockwise until you have plotted all 10 points. Refer to **http://Bonuses.TeamsRock.com** for examples of what the circle might look like.

2. Once you have plotted all eight items with a dot on the wheel, now you want to draw a line and connect all eight dots. If you are lucky, there might be some semblance of a circle (maybe more of an octagon) inside your wheel.

3. Locate the two or three lowest scores, and review these with the employee. The ultimate goal is to enlarge and balance the circle for each employee. The purpose of drawing this out is to visually illustrate for both you and the employee the weaker areas that need to be addressed over the coming months. Once you have discussed and agreed on the low points it is time to establish a plan of action.

4. Now it is time to establish a plan of action. It is now important that you provide the employee any tools they may need to excel in this endeavor. Perhaps they need to take a specific training class, work with another employee as a mentor, or they may actually need a new widget to work better. This does not mean to only focus on the specific items.

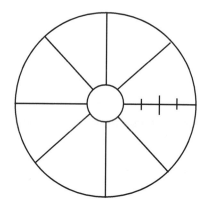

You and the employee will now review this wheel every 90 days. You do not have to start from the beginning each time – simply review the eight items to see that they are still relevant, and update the scoring. After each meeting the employee may have a new set of items to focus on for the subsequent meeting. After each meeting the employee should feel as though they have improved their skill set in those areas.

Every year you should redo the entire process to establish new goals and objectives.

The primary purpose of this process is to establish communication with your employees. By doing this, you build trust and respect, as well as more open conversations with everyone. Each employee may have a different set of goals even if they share similar positions, and that is normal.

If you have been the team leader for a while, it is likely that you already know where your employees need assistance. This is great because now, you can develop a specific plan for training, coaching, and mentoring, as well as the necessary tools the employee may need to become successful.

An additional thought — while you are their leader, it is not essential that you know how to do an employee's specific tasks – it is essential, however, that you know what those tasks are and how to lead them toward success.

✱ Employee Feedback

Before you know where you are going, you must first know where you are, and before you know where you are, you must know from whence you came. This is essential to your development as an effective leader.

Write down the name of your best boss. They may be your current boss or one from many years ago. Next, write down three specific reasons that person was, or is, your best boss. Remember, this does not have to be the person you are currently working for. They can be any boss you've had since you entered the adult workforce.

Best Boss Name

Why they are/were the best:

1_____

2_____

3_____

Use a separate sheet of paper if you think you will give this book to someone else to read later. The key is to write this down.

Take a moment and look at those things that made them a great boss. In my workshops and keynote programs, I almost immediately see the same trend every time. You may have written things like:

* ✱ They trusted me
* ✱ They pushed and challenged me
* ✱ They encouraged me
* ✱ They gave me feedback.

What I do not see is that they did their reports on time. More often than not, it was because they developed and nurtured you as an employee. Your connection to, and nurturing of, your team members not only creates a better employee. It creates loyalty and trust, while at the same time helping them grow. I know this is true for my best boss ever. It is because of him that I am where I am today. That was over 30 years ago. I was in my early 20's and I only worked with Bob for about 18 months. It does not take a long time to make a powerful impact.

When you were in high school, were you ever called to the principal's office? Being called into the boss's office is similar to being called into the principal's office when we were kids. What did you think the first time you got a note to go to the principal's office?

Most people when they are called to the principal's office are thinking, "Oh crap."

For me, it was eleventh grade. It was the fifth period, after lunch and I walked into English class where my teacher handed me a note. It said, "Go see Mr. Tracy in the office."

I looked at my teacher and asked, "What did I do?"

She said, "I don't know. Mr. Tracy just wants to see you."

I went to a fairly large high school and I was all the way at the other end of the building from the office. I took my time walking to that principal's office. I entered the front part of the office where the principals and the vice-principals were and I handed the note to the secretary and timidly said, "I'm supposed to see Mr. Tracy" in a very soft voice.

The secretary replied, "Go on back to his area and his admin is there to help you." I walked back there. Again, I asked, "What did I do?"

She said, "Have a seat Mr. Gregory, Mr. Tracy will be with you in just a moment."

I was scared to death. I had never been called to the principal's office before. Mr. Tracy walked in and said, "Good afternoon, Mr. Gregory. Would you join me in my office?"

Nervous, I stood up and walked slowly into his office and I came right out and said, "I didn't do it."

Mr. Tracy in his forethought and wisdom said, "Mr. Gregory, don't you feel it is important that you know what you are being charged with before you plead innocent or guilty?"

What a concept. I did not know what to say at this point. As a junior in high school, that had a profound impact on me and I've never forgotten it.

"Yeah, I guess so." I replied, with some hesitancy.

"Last week at our homecoming game you were on the committee working with the junior class float. Is that correct?"

"Yes sir," I replied.

"At the last minute there was a problem with the car being able to pull the float in the halftime parade. Is that correct?"

I replied quickly, "Well yeah. It happened right before the game started. We knew we weren't going to be able to get hooked up right."

"And I understand that you went home and got your parents' station wagon and came back up here and hooked the car up and were able to get your junior class float to go in the parade on time and you missed the entire first half of the football game. Is that right?"

"Well, yes sir."

He reached his hand across his desk extended his hand and shook my hand as he said, "Thank you for your school patriotism and your school spirit. I called you down here to let you know how much we appreciate what you did. Now get back to class." Needless to say, I walked back to class with a little skip in my step.

Feedback is not just about the negative. As the leader, if you bring somebody into your office only to have them deal with a bad issue — any time you say, "Bob, can I see you in the office?" Bob is going to know what is coming and so will the rest of the team.

I had one gentleman in a workshop admit, "Whenever I had to deliver bad information I always told the person — let's go for a walk. Everybody started to realize, every time he said, "Let's go for a walk," that something bad was going to happen."

Make sure you are providing positive as well as negative feedback, whether in your office or elsewhere. In today's society, we get stronger responses and reaction with the carrot than we do with the stick. It's fundamental to recognize that. Positive feedback works. Now, don't get me wrong — do not start praising for simple things that are part of the employee's regular duties and responsibilities — like, "Hey Susan, very good, you answered the phone 30 times today." Doing this will simply create an entitlement mentality and a culture within the team that will cause more damage that benefit.

Now, if she's picking up extra duties, or covering for a receptionist — maybe it would be a good idea to offer a little praise. Just don't praise people for doing their job the way they are expected to do. My father used to say, "I'm not here to kiss somebody's butt to get them to do the job they were hired to do in the first place. Sit down, shut up, and work." Yes, my father served in WWII.

Praise your team for the right things. Give them feedback. Let them know that what they are doing is valued. Let them know that they are being appreciated. You can leave them little notes. It doesn't have to be anything of major significance. A great phrase I learned very early in my career is, "Behavior that is rewarded equals behavior that is repeated." So, if you reward average behavior, you will continue to receive average productivity.

Recognition and positive feedback can be as simple as a post-it note that says, "Thanks, I appreciate the work." There are so many things you can do to recognize outstanding behavior.

✳ When It Isn't Good News

Sometimes, you will be faced with giving a different kind of feedback — negative feedback. It is not comfortable for many of us, for we feel that it may trigger conflicts (which it usually does not). While nobody likes giving it or receiving it, it is a necessary part of learning and improving. I have learned more from mistakes that others have told me about than my successes. Negative feedback should be used carefully and thoughtfully, as it really affects your rapport with your entire team - not just the person you are delivering it to.

There are some strategies that can soften the blow and deliver the desired effect of either eliminating a bad behavior (coming into work late) or increasing a positive behavior (increasing your sales or customer satisfaction numbers). The secret is to provide the feedback immediately.

* ✴ ALWAYS provide negative feedback in private. Never shame employees in front of their peers.

* ✴ Open with positive accomplishments and focus on the strengths, not the weak points.

﹡ Do NOT use the word "but" after you deliver the initial positive praise. "But" is an eraser word. It will negate the positive things you just said. Many want to use the word 'however.' I feel that the word 'however' is nothing more than the word 'but' dressed up in a tuxedo. Instead, when you use the word 'and' you actually draw the two thoughts together in a very positive way.

﹡ Use descriptive words

﹡ Avoid using absolute words such as never and always

﹡ Focus on performance and behavior not your judgments

﹡ Ask probing questions to attempt to uncover unknown causes for behavior

﹡ State the specific areas of concern

﹡ Don't focus on what they have no control over

﹡ Be open and accessible for value added support

﹡ Listen with empathy

﹡ Offer assistance for improvement

﹡ Finish the feedback with another positive. Sandwich your remarks with Positive-Negative-Positive comments

﹡ When the person corrects the mistake be sure to let them know they corrected it. Behavior rewarded equals behavior that is repeated

In the next chapter, we will dig even deeper into personality styles and company culture. Creating an environment that is predictable, consistent and welcoming helps connect and create stronger relationships within the team.

Chapter 4 Effectively Leading a team to Success

Effective communication is essential for every leader. It's one of the strongest tools in our toolbox with regard to building trust, garnering respect, gaining commitment, and developing a strong followership.

As a leader, it's imperative that you understand the power of the three Vs (refer back to the team side of the book on page T•50 for more information on the three Vs of communication). Even more imperative for you, as a leader, is understanding how impactful your daily interactions with team members can be.

For instance, suppose you walk by John and say, "Good job." That's it, that is all you say, and you show no emotion in your voice and make minimal eye contact. You are not saying it with conviction and belief. Therefore, John may feel you are being insincere with your comment.

While this may not be true, it is the way your message is inferred by the receiver that is critical. Remember, it is more about them than it is about you. Make sure that your communication skills are strong, especially when giving compliments. It is critical that you match the other person's natural behavior style, and yes, people can feel the difference.

Now, let's take a look at the different behavioral styles of your team, to gain a better understanding of what motivates them the most, and what will turn them off.

Let's stop and think about one of the bestselling books of all time, *How to Win Friends and Influence People* by Dale Carnegie. There's a reason the book has been listed at the top of leadership lists for decades. It's about how you communicate and lead people. You have to know how to go out there and interact with your team. Do you high-five everybody? No. Do you need to kiss everybody's hand?

No. It's about understanding how to work with each person on a unique basis that fits their style.

What works for one person does not work for everyone. Each of us has a preferred communication style. Some people like longer explanations, while others just want you to bottom-line it and get to the point. You may have a team with people all over the place in their personality and communication styles. Your job is to know what those styles are, and what each team member needs. Then, help team members communicate more clearly and effectively with one another.

✳ Leading with Everything DiSC

Wouldn't it be wonderful if you had a secret key or decoder to know, motivate, and develop each member on your team? Well you do have such a decoder. On the team side of this book, I introduced you to Everything DiSC profiles and demonstrated how we are wired to interact with others and how others are wired to interact with us. In the following examples, we will utilize four co-workers on the same team.

* Bottom-line Bob
* Jovial Joanna
* Warm Warren
* Detailed Donna

Let's look at how you can be more effective at delegating, developing and motivating each of these behavior styles.

Delegation:

Bottom-line Bob:

When delegating to Bottom-line Bob, success will come when you communicate with him directly and succinctly. No rambling on or idle chitchat. Just give him enough details to get started. If he needs more information, he will find you. Too much information or idle chitchat, and Bob will tune you out the same way you change the radio station in your car when you hear a song you do not like. Bob's natural Everything DiSC style is a "D".

Jovial Joanna:

If you are too abrupt with a Jovial Joanna, and do not chat with her a bit, she may feel unheard and dismissed, because her natural Everything DiSC style is an "i". Joanna wants and needs attention. She is typically a very positive and energetic person, and likes to communicate with the same energy.

Warm Warren:

Warren simply wants everyone to get along. His natural Everything DiSC style is an "S". Warren does not like to rock the boat and is very consistent in his work. He likes to take his time, think through the process, and explore alternatives. Warren rarely says 'no' to a request to help someone out.

Detailed Donna:

Donna likes, and needs, lots of information. Her natural Everything DiSC style is a "C". If she does not get the details she needs, she will quiz you on what is needed. Donna's primary focus is quality. She takes pride in the quality of the work she produces.

Each style needs to be approached and communicated with differently. It is important for you to know your natural Everything DiSC style because this is your go-to style. In order for you to build trust and respect among the team, you will need to adapt to the style of others, regardless of your natural go-to style.

Successful leaders recognize how critical it is to understand each person's natural style, their chemistry and how they fit into the team.

Motivation:

As we talked about earlier, motivation comes from within and, as the leader, your task is to encourage and give your team a reason to want to continue the positive behavior. Remember, behavior that is rewarded equals behavior that is repeated. With that being said, different styles respond differently to your actions. Here are some suggestions that can help you in the motivation of your team members as it relates to the Everything DiSC behaviors.

Let's start with Jovial Joanna, who likes to be the center of attention, thus public recognition is the key for her. Showing that you value her contribution to the team is essential. If the behavior is significant, preparing a certificate can work nicely.

Conversely, Warm Warren does not like public recognition. In fact, recognition beyond the immediate team may have an adverse effect on Warren. The best way to recognize Warren is to do it in private, maybe even send him a card or a personal email. He will respond favorably to the softer, intrinsic motivators.

As you may have surmised, Detailed Donna is like Warren, and does not prefer public recognition. She is very task and quality driven. One of the most effective ways to recognize Donna is to provide her with an email or letter of commendation. Be sure to let her know that you have copied both senior management and human resources.

Bottom-line Bob is truly self-motivated and quick recognition is a great technique. Another stellar way to reward Bob is to assign him more duties and responsibilities. Note — this does not mean more offloading of work — Bob will appreciate the respect you have given him with the added responsibilities.

Now that you have an idea of the different behavioral styles that can exist within an organization, we are going to shift to the environment within which you and your team work.

Think about a sports team. Each team's coach and players have their own sets of skills, personalities, and ways they play. They have to adapt to each field they compete in. It is assumed that they have an advantage in their home field because it is where they practice and what they know best. The team knows the feel, and they have more confidence, which creates the home field advantage. This translates, in business, as a Knowledge Centered Environment.

✺ Knowledge Centered Environment

When was the last time you were inside a McDonalds? Imagine standing at the counter. Where is the French fry machine? If you said off to the left — you know your McDonald's. Now, find someone who has not been inside a McDonald's in several years and see if they can answer that question. In my workshops, I have found that people who have not been inside of a McDonald's in over 10 years still know where the French fry machine is located. Why after 10 years is someone able to answer an obscure question such as that? It is because McDonald's believes in consistency in every aspect of their business.

Regardless of the industry or business you are in, a fully functional Knowledge-Centered work environment should look and function similar to a McDonald's restaurant. It is predictable and functional. McDonald's builds an organization that is based on knowledge of their systems. Everything is built in a consistent certain way.

Consistency is the key to a Knowledge-Centered Environment. Webster defines consistency as a condition of adhering together. Regardless of where an employee's work takes them, they should experience the same feel and atmosphere as if they were working in the same location day after day. That is what makes organizations successful. They are consistent. Marriott and Google are strong name brands due to the consistency in their business. Chic-fil-A has consistency in the way that they provide service. Every one of these companies has consistency as part of their foundation.

While consistency is easy to recognize in a retail environment and on manufacturing lines, it is a bit more challenging in our offices and in our day-to-day lives.

VDI's

Today, with mobile networks and tele-commuters, consistency is necessary for virtually every business. It is likely that we can be working on our desktops in the office, our laptops, or our personal computer at home and, perhaps, even on a tablet or our smartphones — all within the span of a couple of hours. This can translate into a variety of operating systems.

With this need for mobility, Virtual Desktops (or VDI — virtual desktop infrastructure) are becoming increasingly more popular in organizations so that people can literally pick their desk up and go somewhere else. These companies are using the cloud more often to stay connected.

Heinan Landa (CEO of Optimal Networks Inc.) says that consistency is the key to VDI's. Virtual desktops help increase productivity and keep employees focused on work. A well thought out VDI creates the Virtual Desktop Environment necessary to keep employees and projects on course. They create consistency in the workplace because all computing is done in one place and each person uses their computer as an access point. All computing is uniform and no matter what physical computer you are working on — you are on "your computer." It has the same look, feel, and desktop you are used to seeing and navigating.

These VDIs keep employees focused on the tasks at hand by having one desktop accessible anywhere employees are able to connect. They get to work more quickly with one version of software and with everything stored in the cloud; they always have access to the latest version of documents.

When people move to a virtual environment, mobility is another key benefit. Typically, remote access is convoluted at best. The virtual world cleans that all out and streamlines it to a simple environment. In a virtual environment, even when you are in the office, you are technically working remotely.

Meetings are important whether you all work in the same office or check in virtually. Many times, meetings have no real purpose and take up time. Also, people will avoid them if they don't see value in them.

A virtual desktop environment lays an excellent foundation for a Knowledge Centered Environment, and, the challenge comes with creating the same functionality with the people on a team, or on a variety of teams, within the company.

As the leader, it is your job to ensure the members of your team are balanced and somewhat interchangeable. Processes and systems must be in place and be synchronized.

Think about your company. Is it possible for employees to easily move from team to team or does every team have their own structure? The more consistent the processes are, the more powerful the team. It is critical for everyone to be involved with sharing the knowledge they have with other team members and others across the organization. The stronger the systems you have in place, the more effectively your team can operate.

✸ Effective Meetings

We've all attended a meeting at some point in time that was absolutely useless for us. Yet it was a mandatory, or as I sometimes call it a "Manda-Fricka-Tory" meeting. We've all had mandatory meetings that meant nothing to us. There may have been some value for others on the team or to other divisions, yet there was simply no value to us other than an absolute waste of our time. Another challenge is that many of the meetings we attend are simply boring. As a leader, what we want to make sure of is that the right people are in these meetings, the information is applicable to all attendees, and that information is delivered in a way that will be retained by all attendees. Here are a few key strategies to make your meetings more informative, effective and, of course, more valuable.

Make sure you get the meeting agenda out in advance. Sometimes that's not easy. I recall one time we ended up having an impromptu staff meeting. It wasn't mandatory. We had about eight people who needed to be at the meeting, and were in the office. I had about 30 minutes to prepare the topic of discussion and literally grabbed several large post-it notes and started making an agenda of what needed to be covered. I put them on a piece of paper, went to the copy machine, copied it and had it on the table for everybody when they came into the meeting. An agenda is absolutely critical. Keep in mind that having an agenda is useless unless you stick to it.

Have you ever arrived at a staff meeting on time only to have it begin 10 minutes or more late? Simply start meetings on time. Regardless of whether everybody's in the room or not. You'll gain respect when you do this.

Craig was a new manager who took over a team of about 15 employees. Craig recognized as soon as he was brought onboard that the team naturally went back to the forming stage. Remember, in the forming stage, you need to use a slightly more authoritative style of leadership and ground rules need to be established and expectations set.

Craig always did things a little different, and in this case, he set his first all-hands staff meeting about 10 days in advance. He scheduled the start time for 10:06 A.M. Everybody had plenty of time to know about it, and add it to their calendars. He added it to the master office calendar and actually emailed the agenda two days in advance.

Why 10:06? His thought was that 10:06 was an oddball time and people would be more likely to remember it. On his way into the office that morning, Craig stopped and bought fresh doughnuts and bagels. When he walked into the conference room at 10:06, how many people do you think were present? Now keep in mind, this is his first meeting as the new branch manager.

Nobody was in the conference room. That's right, nobody was there. What did he do? Did he go out to find people? Did he make an office announcement? Did he send out an email? Did Craig do whatever he could do to get people in the office to the meeting? The answer to that is no, he did none of those things. Craig merely started the meeting by talking to an empty room.

Carolyn had an office just across the hall from the conference room. Because she was so close to the conference room, she heard Craig say, "Good morning everybody. Thank you for being here on time. I told you I would not waste your time, and appreciate you not wasting mine. I believe in starting meetings right on time. It is 10:06. Thank you very much for being here." When she heard him begin the meeting, she believed she was the only one who was not in the meeting and immediately went to join the meeting. When Carolyn walked into the conference room, she quickly noticed there was nobody in the room.

Carolyn, now the only person in the room, immediately walked to the far end of the conference table from Craig and sits down, burying her head in her hands. Knowing this is Craig's first meeting; she looked up and thought, "This guy is weird."

Carolyn certainly wasn't going to walk out at this point and, slowly but surely, people started to filter in as Craig continued the meeting.

As the last person came into the meeting room, Craig walked over and closed the door. He then gave the international symbol of time out by holding his hand up in a "T" and said, "If I tell you a meeting starts at 10:06, it means 10:06. It does not mean 10:08. I will allow a two-minute grace period for folks to make our meetings. I am respectful of your time, and I expect you to be respectful of mine and your teammates time as well."

He continued, "At 10:08 the door will be closed. If you are not here by 10:08 don't bother coming in. It is your obligation to get the information on your time if you can't get here on our time." At no point was Craig rude or disrespectful to anyone — just very direct.

Craig definitely utilized a more authoritative style of leadership. When the next meeting started, everyone was there on time. After a couple of weeks, and realizing that a two-minute grace period may not be sufficient, along with the fact that his team included a few sales people and customer service representatives he modified his 2 minute rule. If people were later than two minutes, they could still join the meeting and for every minute beyond 2 minutes, they had to pay 50 cents per minute. Additionally, the last person into the meeting had to take the meeting minutes and have them distributed to everyone within 24 hours. Yes, there was a pre-assigned timekeeper for every meeting. Now, people didn't want to take minutes, now everyone wanted to be early.

Between the late meeting charges along with other ways to generate money, Craig was able to raise about $3,000 in the first year. What did he do with the money?

If you are like most people in my workshops you probably think he bought more doughnuts, or a company picnic.

He did none of the above. Because people assumed at that point that they would be contributing to something for their own fun down the road, Craig donated the money to a local charity.

He made the check out to the charity and invited the charity to the office. He presented them with one of those oversized checks, and then they published the picture in the local newspaper, which brought more publicity and positive outcomes and motivation to the team.

There are some definite strategies to get people to come to meetings and be engaged. They take some preplanning and, more importantly, buy-in from the team. Consider some simple extrinsic motivators to get the team to arrive on time and be ready to talk business. There are a number of books by Bob Pike and Ed Scannell that you can read to help stimulate ideas that will keep your team engaged and happy.

Start on Time and Finish on Time

When you're sending out a note about a meeting, you probably have a pretty good idea how long the meeting should take, assuming you stick to the published agenda. Let's say you're expecting the meeting to take an hour. If you say the meeting will be an hour in the meeting announcement, which allows employees to plan their time. They'll block their calendars accordingly.

If you run about two minutes over, they are going to start to get antsy. What do you do? Follow the customer service philosophy of *Under Promise & Over Deliver*. Theme parks do this better than anyone does. Think about the last time you stood in a long line at a theme park with your kids and saw the sign that said your wait time from that point was 75 minutes. When you get to the front of the line, you realize that your wait was likely significantly less. In this case, simply tell the team that the meeting will be an hour and 15 minutes. Then when the hour is an hour and six minutes, you are a hero because you finished early.

Be Sure the Meeting is at the Right Time for Your Team.

I used to have a boss who would have a meeting every other Friday afternoon at 4 o'clock. Now, in all fairness, he was dealing with sales-people. He did that because he wanted to get people off the golf course.

Did it work? Not a chance. All they did was to go out and golf early in the morning, come back in for the staff meeting. If you have a group of people who are mostly night folks, you don't want to have a meeting at 8:00 in the morning. They are not going to be mentally present. Likewise, if you have morning people, you don't want to have your meeting late in the afternoon. You have to find a time that is physically right to have the meeting.

In most cases, the most effective time to hold a staff meeting is between 10:00 and 11:00 in the morning, right before lunch. The morning people are still going strong, the midday people have ramped up, and the night people are getting started. All bases covered.

When you are conducting multiple meetings across multiple time zones along with virtual meetings, you are probably more cognizant of the time of the meeting. Successful leaders know when most people's peak time is, and schedule meetings accordingly.

Get a Timekeeper

The National Speakers Association has timekeepers at their convention for both the keynote speeches and the breakout sessions. In my keynote speeches, I keep a clock in front of me, or at least find a timekeeper in my audience. In my workshops and training sessions, I watch the time very closely. It's critical that I end on time.

Starting a Meeting

When possible, begin with something different to energize participants.

Professional speakers often open up a presentation with a story, a historical fact, or an amazing statistic. Whatever you choose to use, it needs to be relevant to the topic of the meeting or the company. Using something useless is exactly that, useless. Try to have some kind of an opener for your meetings.

Appropriate Place for Meeting

You don't want to hold your meeting near the lunchroom while everybody else in the company is having lunch. Find appropriate places. When the weather is nice, one of my clients holds their meeting outdoors. Another client has a meeting at the Starbucks in the lobby of their building. There is no perfect place — just the perfect place for the next meeting.

Have a Standup Meeting

It is exactly as it sounds, everybody stands. Guess what, your meetings will go a lot faster and be more on-point. There is no need to have people sitting at desks or at a conference table. Or, you can take chairs into an open bullpen area and sit in a circle. These techniques help break down barriers. When you are standing, or sitting without tables, distractions are minimized and you avoid any "head of table" issues.

Rotate the Facilitator

As the leader, when you always lead the meeting you are going to get into a routine. It's just going to happen. When you get other folks engaged to lead the meeting you are starting to groom them for potential leadership positions. You are giving them skills at practicing and speaking in front of others, the ability to set an agenda, and an understanding of how to set things up. You, as the leader, can still have input for them. If it's a regular weekly meeting that you are having, this is a perfect opportunity to rotate people. One sidebar benefit is that you see who might be a great future leader within the organization. After all, you get to see them prepare and run a meeting.

Create a Parking Lot and Recap the Meeting

This is a simple technique used by professional facilitators, and a place for any topics that are not on the agenda. If you have time, you can address at this meeting or schedule and carry over to the next meeting.

A "parking lot" is a space on the wall or on a table for team members to put post-it-notes with questions, comments, and concerns, not specifically addressed by the agenda for the current meeting.

Recapping the meeting is important. Take time to review any specific assignments for key individuals and make sure everyone knows who is responsible for which tasks.

All of the leadership skills you may apply have limits on their effectiveness. In the end, it is the team and company culture that really engages team members. It is something that is constantly assessed and reviewed by leaders — not only to assess whether the components of the company culture are still relevant, they need to make sure that it has the desired results among team members. They are engaged, they are motivated, they are loyal, and they are dedicated.

✳ Avoiding LRS — The Lone Ranger Syndrome

In a time where we are all being told to do more with less, getting new employees on the team can be wonderful. It can lessen the workload for everyone, increase morale, and create a new way of seeing the same old projects. Yet, getting a new hire up to speed can sometimes be a challenge. There are all types of issues to consider such as their communication style, their skill and will sets, and their assimilation into a team, which could send the team back to the "forming stage.

The idea here is above and beyond what your organization may do regarding the onboarding process. These ideas are for the new employee's first day with the team.

There are ways to make sure that the first day for a new employee is a positive one, so that they feel welcome and so that they do not feel like they are on their own (basically a Lone Ranger). Preparing for their first day also allows them to tap into the Knowledge Centered Environment. You create a routine, from day one, that they can be comfortable with and that allows them to interact quickly with their teammates and begin to work at full steam more quickly and efficiently.

LRS typically sets in right after a new person is hired. The new hire feels as though they have been left alone on an island. A classic example was my first job selling real estate. The first day after I returned from the corporate franchise training my boss basically said, here is your desk, your business cards and your phone. Good Luck. I was on my own right from the beginning. Here are a few simple strategies to help you and your team avoid LRS.

The work begins even before the first day. Get with your IT department and order all of the necessary (albeit it temporary) passwords, and setups so everything is ready on day one. This way, when they arrive, they can hit the ground feeling as if they are part of something and not just going through hoops.

As the team leader, it is important to make sure you sit down with them on their first day, at the very beginning of the day and again at the very end of the day, for a short 10 – 15 minute talk. In the morning meeting, you set up their day and let them know what to expect. The end of the day meeting is an opportunity for you to get feedback and show interest in their success. In many cases, you may be the only person they have met on the team before today. Spending just a few minutes with them will go a long way toward helping build trust.

It's very important that when you bring somebody new onto the team, that you acclimate them right away. We all know what it's been like when we have joined a new group, moved to a new neighborhood, or been the new kid in class. It's tough for anyone.

Building a foundation of trust with a new hire is critical. The best tool for avoiding LRS is learning their behavior style by using the Everything DiSC model. This helps you get a better feel about how they will fit. It is important to understand that the Everything DiSC assessment should never be used as the basis of hiring. It should only be used after a person has accepted a position to help with the onboarding process, employee development, and team building.

The first thing you want to be thinking about once they are on the team is who would be a good mentor for them. When you bring on somebody new to your team, how do you make sure that they don't feel like they are lost out there in Never-never Land? One of the most effective ways is to assign them a mentor. This has an impact on both the new hire and the mentor.

The new hire feels welcome and they will already have an advisor on the team who can show them the ropes and point out all of the nuances of the office or work area. This is even more important if they are relocating from a different part of the country.

The second benefit is that the mentor feels empowered. Some might think that, by having a current team member mentor the new hire, this is just dumping work on an already overworked staff. Rest assured, it is not. With the right team culture and the right community spirit, the results are amazing and no one will think of it as a burden. In fact, the mentor will actually grow from the experience.

In college, I was not a good student. One exception was my freshman algebra class. I was doing well enough that the teacher's assistant (TA) suggested that I tutor a few students. I was shocked. I had NEVER been a tutor before. I was usually on the other side of the tutoring table. By becoming the tutor it forced me to work a little harder and my strong "B" in the class moved up to a solid "A".

In fact, it was one of the only "A's" I ever received. When someone agrees to mentor another employee, it creates a win-win situation. In reality, it is a win-win-win because the team also wins.

There is an additional benefit, because assigning a mentor takes a big burden off your shoulders.

The next way to avoid LRS, is to make sure that the new hire's work area is set up for them before their first day. Clean the work area. Disinfect the telephone. Wipe down the keyboard. Have everything done and cleaned up so that it's literally spotless. If there are drawers in the cubicle, pull them out. Make sure you get a little micro vacuum or wipe out and get all the salt out of the drawers. Let's face it, we've all put salt in one of those drawers at one time or another.

This may sound trivial and all I can say is that one time when we did that for a processor coming on to our team. We wiped down the desk. We cleaned it all out. Made it look new, we didn't have new furniture. These were desks, not cubicle modules. Some of them were beat up. So we made them look as nice as we could. I pulled the desk out from the wall to pick up anything that may have fallen down and, lo and behold, there was a chicken wing back there. Isn't it better that you find this out than having the new hire find it?

One final reminder to help avoid LRS; at the end of their first day, sit down with them and let them talk about their day, as we discussed earlier. Don't miss this simple step, It is human nature for someone to want to know that they are valued and taking an additional few minutes to hear about their day will go far beyond what you might expect.

Now, if your team has taken the Everything DiSC profile assessment, your team is leaps and bounds ahead of others. Once your entire team has taken the profile, each person has access to an Everything DiSC comparison report for anyone else on the team who has taken the assessment. You can even have the members that work together closely and more often create Everything DiSC comparison reports with each other. This comparison report is a very specific report for two individuals which compares and contrasts their natural behaviors and ways that both can adapt and work more effectively together.

Make sure the new hire takes the assessment and let everyone on the team know. Then process the information and teach the new employee how they can better interact with others, including yourself, by using the profile and comparison reports.

If you want to know more about Everything DiSC Comparison Reports go to **http://bonuses.teamsrock.com**

As we discussed on the team side of this book, even with the best of intentions, conflict will arise. Conflict, in and of itself, is actually a good thing — when it is around ideas. Let's face it, if we always agreed on everything, life would be boring. Conflict is a natural part of the growth of every team. The challenge arises when that conflict becomes personal, especially when it is between employees. You may be called upon to handle it judiciously and not only deescalate the situation, but turn it into a team growth experience.

Managing Conflict Like a Champ

As a successful leader, you will need to develop all types of employees. You must be versatile and be prepared to work with a variety of conflict styles that will emerge within your team. Below is a list of recognizable conflict types you may encounter. To work effectively with each type, it is critical that you understand what motivates them and work with them, individually and accordingly.

> *"People are not difficult. They're just different, we make them difficult. It is up to us to work with them and their style."*
>
> **—JOE GILLIAM**

The Bull

You may have heard the expression about the proverbial bull in the china shop. They are so large and unyielding that they would destroy all the breakables just by walking casually through.

The truth is that this is a myth. In one episode of the Discovery Channel show *Myth Busters*, the hosts created an outdoor china shop and allowed the bull to walk through. The bull never knocked anything over or broke anything.

The best and most powerful strategy is to let these people vent. Let them decompress. They will come up for air. If you have ever used a pressure cooker, you know that there is a valve that lets off steam so that the vessel does not explode. In working with the bull, you may have to be that valve and allow the pressure to be released in a controlled manner. If you attack them head on, that could result in someone getting hurt, emotionally or physically.

When they do come up for air, ask them questions. Open-ended questions work best as they engage both sides in conversation. Avoid telling them to calm down. In fact, NEVER tell anyone to calm down. Instead, describe their behavior. I talked about this earlier when I described the boss that exploded because our hotel rooms weren't ready. The receptionist just let him vent and then solved the issue.

The Fox

In nature, the fox is a nocturnal creature. Growing up, I used to hear the phrase, "If you see a nocturnal creature such as a fox or a raccoon during the day, it means that they're rabid." I've since learned that is not the case. If you see a nocturnal creature during the day, and they see you and run away, they are not necessarily rabid. On the other hand, if they don't appear to be afraid of you, then they are more likely to be rabid. What does this mean about team members with the attributes of a fox? This type of person likes to hide and stay back. They are generally passive-aggressive. An exaggerated example of passive-aggressive behavior is someone saying, "Bob, that is a nice tie. Did you get it from a yard sale or a thrift store?" Passive-aggressive types tend to compliment up front and then hit you with a zinger.

Because the fox typically likes to hide, one of the most effective methods of dealing with them is to get them out into the open, to flush out their situation. If you have somebody who's darting around saying innuendos, backing down, not really speaking up in a meeting, and just saying things behind backs, then you probably have a fox on your team. As a leader, you have to bring those issues out into the open, get them out. For instance, "Bob, the other day I heard you talking about _____, would you like to elaborate on that?" By engaging with a question and bringing the topic to the forefront, Bob's true beliefs will be out in the open for the entire team and he is less likely to be defensive.

It is important not to scold them, or talk down to them. If you are correcting them, make sure you are doing this in private. Be sure to ask many open-ended questions to keep them engaged. Bring up ideas to get them to talk. Again, engaging your employees in conversations is a good thing. Successful leaders do not fear this type of conversation. It is vital that you always have to stick to the facts and hold them accountable. Most importantly, when dealing with a fox, stand your ground.

The Whiner

You can recognize a whiner by the whiny sound of their voice. They're complaining, not about major problems, but lots of little things. "I need more help. Bob's not pulling his weight." They talk about being overwhelmed all the time and they're quite vocal in their persistent complaining. Have you ever noticed that the person whining about how busy they are is almost never as busy as others who do not whine?

> *"Look at a day when you are supremely satisfied at the end. It's not a day when you lounged around doing nothing; it's a day you have had everything to do and you've done it."*
>
> **—MARGARET THATCHER**

What the whiner is looking for is empathy. Now, the secret here is to give them some. The operative word is 'some'. Don't give them too much. If you give them too much empathy, you will encourage them to do more whining. While agreeing with them on something can benefit the situation, do not agree with them on everything. When they start whining to you, become a good listener. You can say, "I hear what you're saying. I understand what you're saying." At the end of the day, they will thank you for listening. At least they will feel their voice has been heard and this is a vital step in the overall process of creating a cohesive team. The biggest thing here is you have to be patient.

They will have a tendency to get off track and you need to keep them on track. While acknowledging what they have said, when you finish a conversation with them, you can say, "I need you to get back on task here."

The Deadbeat

It could be that you have an employee that is ripe for retirement. They are just counting down the days. They may even have a countdown calendar on their computer or wall. They feel completely entitled and do just enough to get by.

How do you handle this person? Engage them as often as possible. Continually raise their bar — ever so slightly. Find out what it is that excites them on both a professional and personal level. Be careful not to simply dump more work on them, because that's just going to turn them into a whiner. Don't raise your voice to them as that may turn them into a bull. Find out what it is that excites them about coming to work. Do they enjoy coming to work? If not, why not? What are they missing at work that would really make them excited about coming to work? It is possible they are just a CR 3 — do you remember that? They are quite possibly burned out — either on your team, with their work, or perhaps with the entire organization. Let's face it, they are dragging down the rest of the team and your challenge is to either stimulate them or find a way to move them out.

The Know it All

There are really two types of know it alls: the real and the fake. The first thing you must do is to find out if you're dealing with a real know it all or a fake one. How do you do that? Simply ask factually based questions.

In today's world, we all know it is possible that somebody on your team could be much younger than you or much older than you, come from a different walk of life or live down the street, and know something that you don't know. A confident and secure leader is completely open and not intimated by this person.

Once you determine you're dealing with a fake know it all, the first thing to do is to allow that person to save face. Failing to allow them to save face diminishes the trust you have worked so hard to establish.

Allowing them to save face is as simple as saying, "Sally, not a problem. Don't worry about that. You know a lot of people in the past have felt the same way. A lot of people in the past have made similar mistakes." If you can cite a time you have made a similar mistake, all the better.

When you allow them to save face, you increase your trust quotient. If you do not allow them to save face, more than likely, they will become either the whiner or the bull. Allowing them to save face is going to win them back to your way of thinking. Show them that you care and are not just trying to put them down or one up them.

Now, let's suppose you're dealing with a real know it all. A successful leader welcomes this person's input to the team. Remember, it is quite probable that somebody on your team knows more than you. Secure leaders recognize this and are open to having conversations with this person, and let them know you value them and that they are important to the team. The conversation might go like this, "Bob, you are an integral part of this team, and our team needs you and your experience. Can I count on you for your support?" By doing this, you are showing you acknowledge them and their skills. At this point, do not say another word. Let me repeat that — DO NOT SPEAK!

At this point Bob may turn to you say, "Well I don't know, I'm not a . . ."

You then need to be decisive and assertive and say - "Bob, can I count on you for your support?" Then wait for an answer.

Do not move forward until you get a yes or a no from this person. Odds are that even if this takes three or four times, you are going to get a yes. On the other hand, if you get a no, you now know what you're dealing with, and that's okay too. It's the wishy washy in between, the uncertainty, that causes the problem. Top sales professionals will often tell you they want a yes and that they can handle the rejection of a no. What they hate to hear is, "let me think it over."

To help engage them, you might want to have the know it all take a point position on a project they have significant knowledge about. By doing that, you're showing that you respect them. When you show them you respect them, they will likely show some respect back to you.

The Procrastinator

We will talk about this person later...

Just kidding...

We all procrastinate to some level. Why? One reason that most of us procrastinate, is fear. I learned an acronym for F.E.A.R. from the great Zig Ziglar:

> False
> Evidence
> Appearing
> Real

We don't want to do certain things, because we have a fear. This fear could be a positive fear or negative fear. Some people actually fear success. They fear how people might perceive them if they are successful and how they might be treated. Or what others will say about their success.

The fear of failure is more common, and may manifest itself with phrases like, "It's going to be hard," or "it's too much work." They may even say, and believe, that they do not have the skills, when in fact, you know they do.

The procrastinator is going to put things off until the last minute. They're jumping through hoops trying to get something accomplished. How do you handle them? The best way to handle a procrastinator is give them plenty of time when you delegate a task. The key thing with a procrastinator is to make sure you schedule interim checkpoints, and stay on top of them. Yes, there are some people that need a little micromanaging. You will likely need to stay on top of this person more than others on your team. Another point to remember is to not overwhelm them, as they may become easily overwhelmed. You can also partner them with another team member who does not procrastinate.

In some instances, you may even give them an earlier deadline to ensure you have the task completed in a timely manner. Be careful here – and do not rely on this method; they will eventually figure out what you are doing and adjust their schedule accordingly.

If you know that you have a procrastinator on your team, give them simple tasks and simple decisions, and be sure to appropriately recognize the fact that they met their deadline. When talking with them, give them alternate choice questions. Don't give them too much to think about. A simple choice between A or B is most effective. Then, at each decision stage, make sure you gain their agreement before moving forward.

Think about the restaurant The Cheesecake Factory. I personally struggle going there because there are so many choices. It can take a long time to decide what I want. The concept of fewer choices applies well when dealing with a procrastinator at work. Never give more than three choices and preferably only two.

The Bulldog

The bulldog is somebody who typically just tears into something. When they get their teeth into it, they won't let it go, whether it's a challenge, a problem, or a project. They become obsessed with working on this one thing. Some might call it tunnel vision. When communicating with others, they will latch onto one comment or idea and not let it go. They tend to interrupt, not listen and continue to go back to that one idea. Again, engaging them in healthy conversation is the most effective technique. Continue asking a series of open-ended questions that take them down a pre-determined path.

An example of an open-ended question to change the direction or topic might be, "What are your thoughts about…?" This type of question puts the onus on them to come up with an answer and will change their focus from the idea they may be obsessing about.

Be supportive of their needs and be persistent in what you want from them. Go back and rearticulate the needs or goals of the project, the process, the team, or whatever it happens to be.

One of the greatest tools you have in your toolbox as a leader is effective communication and, within communication, one of your greatest assets is silence. When I first started in the mortgage banking industry in 1983, my first senior Vice President, used to say, "You have two eyes, two ears, and one mouth, so that you can do twice as much watching and listening, as you do speaking." That philosophy has helped me immensely over the years.

The Time Bomb

The typical characteristics of the time bomb are that, in many situations, you never know when, how, or what will set them off. They are diligently working on a task and the next thing you know ---- BOOM. They've just blown up. We typically know who they are and, too often, we just walk on eggshells around them trying not to set them off. So how do we handle the time bomb?

In reality, there are some signals or indicators that they might be about to go ballistic. They'll start to have rapid breathing and deeper sighs. S-I-G-H-S. They may possibly roll their eyes.

Next, their words will start to get short. They will start speaking in three and four word sentences. The voice modulation will tend downward at that end of the sentence. You begin to sense their frustration.

Finally, their volume goes up and they begin to yell and scream, followed by swearing and foul language.

How do you handle them? Try to keep them in the first or even second phase by showing empathy and listening to them. Recognize and understand what they're saying, and find one thing to agree with them on. This will allow them to release some pressure without a full blow up.

Now, if you're getting them at the third stage when they've already blown up, you treat them just as you would a bull. Let them vent, let them come up for air, let them talk it through, and again, find one thing you can find a common ground on. Do not agree on everything. Pick one thing.

The goal is to diffuse the situation before it escalates to the next level. In the team side of the book, we talked about the three stages of conflict that can occur. You may want to review them.

Remember, as a leader, you must stay calm, control the situation, and steer it to a successful resolution. Don't seek to control or dominate the other person, as this rarely works. Keep your voice steady. Not too loud, not too soft. You will be able to handle any conflict like a true champ!

✹ Final Thoughts

Congratulations, you made it to the end of the leader side of the book! You now have the right tools for building a winning team. As I mentioned early in the book, a ship needs a strong and trustworthy captain to get its cargo and crew to their destination.

My hope is that you have begun to find your course and learn how to steer your team towards its goals. By recognizing how you chart your course, preparing for challenges, and making the necessary changes, you can help navigate your team toward growth, success, and longevity.

For individual days, and because good days are for average people; first remember that you are not average; so make today a:

Magnificent or Marvelous Monday
Terrific Tuesday
Wonderful, Wacky Wednesday
Thriving and Tremendous Thursday
Fantastic or Fabulous Friday
Superlative Saturday
Sensational Sunday

Use the above to set you and your team apart from others in your organization and feel free to make up your own, and never settle for an average day again.

At **Teams Rock**, we are about the team, and the 'WE' not the 'I', so make sure you have a **"We-Markable Week."**

T   Success begins with **TRUST**

E   Results "happen" with **ENGAGEMENT**

A   Mutual **ACCOUNTABILITY**

M   Passion for the **MISSION**

S   **SYNCHRONIZE** across lines

R   Focus on **RESULTS**

O   100% **OWNERSHIP** of actions

C   **CULTURE** is core

K   Share your **KNOWLEDGE**

Made in the USA
Columbia, SC
01 December 2018